Ea

Sports Nutrition for
Runners and Triathletes

By Chrissy Carroll, MPH, RD, LDN

Dedication: To my wonderful hubby, who races alongside me – thanks for putting up with me as I spent countless nights writing this.

Common Questions

Answers to Common Questions

In writing this, I'm anticipating a few common questions simply about the book's style and content. I want to address them now, so you're prepared throughout the rest of the book!

Why did you focus so much of the book on everyday eating?
Because without a proper everyday eating plan, you won't see the most success in your training, leading to poor race outcomes. Training + Everyday Athlete Diet + Proper Exercise Fueling = Successful Performance. You need all the components, not just the race-day plan.

Why the heck did you list everything in kilograms?
Sorry, guys – just about every study or book on this topic uses kilograms; it's the standard. If I converted everything to pounds, and you decided to look into other books or visit some of the research studies provided in the references, it could easily get confusing going back and forth between the two. So, I used kilograms as the standard throughout most of the book. It's a pretty easy calculation (your weight divided by 2.2) and you only need to figure it out once for all the calculations.

Why do you cite studies that only have 10 people? Isn't that frowned upon?
In normal scientific research, we want large sample sizes because it helps better support a possible conclusion/connection. However, the research on endurance athletes is almost always done with a small group (five to twenty participants). Why? There simply aren't that many endurance athletes out there! Less than 1 percent of the population has ever run a marathon, and while the statistics aren't as clear on triathlons, the numbers seem to indicate around 7 to 14 percent of the population has completed one of any distance (from sprint to ironman). Now jumping back to the research – when you try to get a group of people to participate in multiple

trials comparing different training methods or nutrition protocols, it's going to be difficult to find a large group who a) are athletes in the running/triathlon community, and b) are willing to take the time to complete the study. This leads to very small research studies on endurance sports. We have to make do with what's out there and draw the best conclusions possible based on the body of research available.

TL;DR? I'm lost.
TL;DR is an internet acronym standing for "too long; didn't read." My husband loves Reddit, and they use it all the time on there, so of course, now he's got me using it. At the end of some sections, you'll notice a "TL;DR tip section" where I highlight the most important concepts. It's very helpful if you're skimming the book and looking for a quick answer.

I loved this book, but I need more guidance. What should I do?
Because sports nutrition is so individualized, it's hard to give exact guidelines in a book. If you're not sure how to do the calculations presented or feel overwhelmed implementing these concepts, simply a) follow the food based advice, like eating meals rich in healthy carbohydrates, adequate protein, and moderate amounts of fat, or b) work with a sports dietitian who can give you individualized advice. Through phone and Skype based sessions, I'm able to work with clients all over the United States, so feel free to reach out to me for individualized guidance. There are also many other fantastic sports dietitians out there who may be local to you.

Nutrition & Performance

Nutrition & Performance

As an athlete, you are no doubt used to committing time and energy to your sport, whether that is distance running or triathlon (or both!). Developing a stellar nutrition plan can be a key piece to your training – whether you're a competitive racer looking to up level your performance, or you're a weekend warrior who is just tired of feeling gastrointestinal upset on every run. A proper everyday training diet combined with a great race day fueling plan will serve you well in optimizing your performance and physical comfort.

Why worry about nutrition and fueling? Consider these six benefits of creating a healthy nutrition plan:

1. Provides essential nutrients for your body, including macronutrients (carbohydrates, fat, and protein) and micronutrients (vitamins and minerals), plus the "extras" like antioxidants and phytochemicals
2. Supports your immune system (I'm sure the last thing you want is to get sick during your training season)
3. Helps you maintain a healthy body weight
4. Supports training and your ability to continue training over long periods of time
5. Maximizes performance during races
6. Assists with recovery after training and racing

What's amazing about endurance nutrition is there is quite a bit of consistent research out there that provides us with guidelines on how to optimize our nutrition and fueling plans! I'll mention some of the studies throughout this book and provide you tons of references at the end, in case you're a nerdy science-geek like me and enjoy reading that stuff.

Now, you may be thinking, "Okay, okay, it's important. But how much of a difference will it really make?" Well, consider this simple example that has to do with fueling during exercise. Note that when this is combined with proper everyday nutrition during training, the results can be maximized even further.

A study looked at 18 endurance trained cyclists and compared athletic performance during two cycling time trials on two different days (Hottenrott et al, 2012). The activity involved two and a half hours of moderate intensity cycling, followed by five minutes of rest, and then a 40 mile time trial. During one of the time trials, a scientifically based nutrition strategy was used. During the other trial, the athlete chose their own nutrition strategy as they pleased. For the first time trial, half the athletes completed the scientific strategy first, while half completed the athlete's choice strategy first. On the second occasion, each athlete completed whatever strategy they didn't do the first time.

The scientific strategy used in this study was based on conclusions and recommendations from many different peer reviewed journal articles. It included 500 mg of sodium per liter of fluid, 90 grams of carbohydrate per hour (60 grams of glucose and 30 grams of fructose – a 2:1 glucose:fructose ratio), and 5 mg of caffeine per kilogram of body weight.

Quick aside: If you're feeling overwhelmed looking at those numbers and worried that this is all too scientific, don't worry. I'm going to break down all the recommendations and information on each of these different topics. For now, just be aware that those numbers are based on research, while the athletes' choices may not be.

The results of the study?
- During the two and a half hours of cycling done in advance of the time trial, fluid, carbohydrate, and sodium intake were higher in the scientific approach compared to the athlete's choice approach. This is not a surprise to me, as I

find that many athletes training for long endurance races (those over two and a half hours) tend to under fuel.

- There was a significantly larger power output using the scientific strategy compared to the athlete's choice strategy – 212 vs. 184 Watts.
- The scientific nutrition strategy resulted in a significantly faster time trial – an average of 128 minutes compared to 136 minutes (eight minutes faster!). That's a pretty big difference whether you're trying to podium or simply PR in a race.

Besides training, natural ability, and race conditions (extreme heat or cold, for example), dietary factors are one of the only other factors that have been consistently associated with endurance athlete performance. For example, among a group of novice marathoners, the only thing that predicted marathon time aside from a 2 mile time trial (which of course, indicates pace and ability) was the athletes' day-before and morning-of carbohydrate intake (Wilson et al, 2012). The carbohydrate intake leading up to the race accounted for as much as 4 percent of differences in time. Let's say you're completing an Olympic Distance triathlon in around three hours – that 4 percent difference could mean crossing the finish line up to seven minutes faster! Or if you are a four-hour marathoner who hasn't paid much attention to your fueling, incorporating proper nutrition strategies could mean about 10 minutes shaved off your time!

And aside from the scientific research, both myself and many of my clients have personally experienced improved performance with better nutrition. My greatest triumph comes from an improvement in my marathon times.

When I ran the Maui Marathon in 2010, I knew what the race day nutrition recommendations were but I didn't put them into place very well. So despite following my workout schedule "to a T" throughout training, I ended up under-fueling during the race, which significantly impacted my performance. I felt exhausted by mile 16 – not a great place to be hitting the wall – not to mention throwing up several times during the race. I finished seven minutes over my goal time.

A year later I ran the Cleveland Marathon. I had several hiccups in my training plan, including two missed long runs due to a bad case of the flu. However, I put a much more structured race-day fueling plan in place. During that race I felt entirely more energized, didn't "hit the wall" until mile 23 or 24, and finished 15 minutes faster than my Maui race. Now, of course the race conditions (extreme heat in Maui versus cold in Cleveland) played a partial role in that, but the race day fueling contributed as well.

The take home message here is that it's important to learn about the nutrition recommendations that are available and that have been shown in research to be optimal. And kudos to you, because you're obviously working to learn those things through the purchase of this book!

Energy Needs & Weight

Energy Needs & Weight

Many times when I work with clients, they want to jump right into their race day fueling strategy. And while I'm so excited to help them nail down a race-day plan, there are many other components to a nutrition plan that should be in place before race day. Let's start with the basics – calorie needs and healthy weight ranges for athletes.

If you look at food labels on packages, if you've ever worked on weight management, or if you've read any type of health magazine, you've no doubt read about the calories in food. But what are calories? They are actually a unit of energy. In science speak, 1 calorie is the amount of energy it takes to raise the temperature of 1 gram of water by 1 degree Celsius.

Calories come from three macronutrients – protein, carbohydrate and fat. There are also calories in alcohol. Check out the number of calories per gram of each:
- 1 gram of protein = 4 calories
- 1 gram of carbohydrate = 4 calories
- 1 gram of fat = 9 calories
- 1 gram of alcohol = 7 calories

When you hear the common myth that "fat makes you fat," the root of this is typically based on the fact that fat has the most calories per gram compared to carbohydrates and protein. This is true, but fat also helps you feel full and satiated at meals. So even though healthy fats are rich in calories, you may not need as much of them to feel full. A moderate amount of fat is certainly an important part of an athlete's diet.

How many calories do I need?

As human beings, we need calories to provide us with energy to keep our bodies functioning. Each cell process, our heart beating, our muscles contracting – they all require energy.

Athletes often require more calories than the general population. This makes sense because, as an athlete, you are doing a significant amount of cardiovascular exercise each week which burns many calories. In addition, athletes often have a greater proportion of muscle mass – and the more muscle mass you have, the more calories you burn just sitting around.

The specific amount of calories your body needs varies based on many factors. Age, gender, medical conditions, physical activity level (like every day walking, moving around at work, etc.) and exercise routines (structured training) all affect the number of calories your body burns and thus how much you should take in. Genetics also plays a role, with some individuals just having a slower or faster metabolism than others. Most adults need somewhere between 1,500 calories and 2,800 calories. However, athletes may need anywhere from 1,700 to 4,000+ calories depending on their level of training.

You can estimate the number of calories you need each day using several different calculations. Each equation uses an initial step to determine resting energy expenditure – or the number of calories your body burns each day at rest just keeping you alive – and then uses a second step called an "activity factor." Most activity factors are based on both your everyday activity (like if you walk around a lot at work versus sitting at a desk all day), as well as your exercise regimen. This will give you the number of calories you need to maintain your current weight.

Remember that calculations are simply estimates, and are not perfect for everyone. They will no doubt overestimate energy needs for some people and underestimate energy needs for others. However, they are a great starting place if you are interested in trying to figure out your daily calorie needs.

I've provided two different equations below, and there are <u>practice worksheets in the appendix</u> for you to figure out your own needs. You can use the quick and simple method for an easy (but less accurate) estimate, or you can work through the Mifflin equation for a more specific estimate. Note that you'll need to convert your weight to kilograms for these, which you can do by dividing your weight in pounds by 2.2.

Quick & Simple (easiest method but sometimes less accurate):

Step 1: Determine resting energy expenditure
Men: Weight in kilograms x 24
Women: Weight in kilograms x 22

Step 2: Determine total calorie needs using activity factor
Multiply by activity factor
X 1.2 for sedentary day/job and/or little physical activity
X 1.3 for a few days of light activity
X 1.5-1.6 for up to 1 hour of moderate to intense physical activity/day
X 1.7 for 1-2 hours of moderate to intense physical activity/day
X 1.9-2.1 for very active job (construction worker for example), full time athletes, and/or multiple hours of physical activity everyday

Mifflin Equation:

Step 1: Determine resting energy expenditure
Men: $(10 \times wt\ in\ kg) + (6.25 \times ht\ in\ cm) - (5 \times age) + 5$
Women: $(10 \times wt\ in\ kg) + (6.25 \times ht\ in\ cm) - (5 \times age) - 161$

Step 2: Determine total calorie needs using activity factor
Multiply by activity factor:
X 1.2 for sedentary
X 1.375 for light activity (1-3x/week)
X 1.55 for moderate activity (3-5x/week or more days at an easier intensity)
X 1.75 for heavy activity (6-7x/week)
X 1.9 to 2.1 very heavy (exerting job; two-a-days; full time athletes)

Alternative Method: Estimating Your Baseline
If you hate calculations or if you feel that they are giving you a number quite different than what you expected (which is certainly possible given the fact that other factors like genetics can play a role in metabolic rate), you can also try tracking your intake for several days to garner an estimate of how many calories you need. Websites like SuperTracker, MyFitnessPal, FitDay, or Lose It are all food trackers available for free online. Ignore the calorie recommendations given on these sites (they're often inaccurate, particularly for athletes – although SuperTracker will likely give you the best estimate), and just track your own normal intake. Average several days together to get an estimate of about how many calories you are currently taking in. If you're maintaining a steady weight, this is approximately how many calories your body is using each day.

Alternative Method: Metabolic Rate Assessment
There are more accurate ways to estimate your caloric needs, though. You can have your metabolic rate measured at some hospital labs, exercise physiology labs, and even through some dietitians. This can be expensive, though. Generally, you can use equations or food records to come up with an estimate of your needs and then troubleshoot from there fairly quickly. However, if you've been struggling with losing weight for a long time despite cutting calories to a moderate level, or you seem to be eating continuously yet losing weight – and you are concerned about the

impact that this is having on your performance – then it may be appropriate to search out a facility that offers metabolic testing.

Am I at a healthy weight?

The equations and methods listed above will provide you with an idea of how many calories you need each day to maintain your current weight. However, many runners and triathletes are concerned about their current weight. They may feel they need to lose or gain weight, and often for good reason. Eating too much can lead to excess body weight, which puts more pressure on your joints during running and can make it more difficult to power up hills when cycling. Cutting calories too low and dropping into an unhealthy underweight range can also mean you're losing lean muscle mass, resulting in less ability to power through workouts. If you are concerned about your weight, there are several ways of assessing if you are in a healthy range, which can help you to figure out if you're eating the right amount of calories.

BMI
BMI, or body mass index, is a calculation that compares your weight to your height. You can find out your BMI using an online table or calculator, or using the calculation worksheet in the appendix. Your BMI can be compared to these categories to determine your weight status:

BMI Calculation	Classification
<18.5	Underweight
18.5–24.9	Normal Weight
25–29.9	Overweight
30 or greater	Obese

If you fall into the overweight and obese categories, there are increased health risks for heart disease and diabetes. Falling in the underweight category can also increase the risk of certain health problems.

BMI does have some limitations, though. It can overestimate fat in those who are very muscular and underestimate fat in older people who have lost muscle. For example, if you are very athletic with a lot of muscle mass, your BMI may put you in the "overweight" range but you may actually be at a healthy weight for your body. It's also been suggested that certain ethnicities have different BMI cutoffs when evaluating disease risk. For example, people of Asian descent show increased risk for type 2 diabetes and cardiovascular disease at a BMI of 23 rather than 25 (WHO, 2004).

Weight/Clothes
Looking at your weight by itself without considering your height won't provide you with as much information as BMI. A weight of 160 pounds may be healthy for a tall female, but not healthy for someone who is only 5'1". BMI helps you figure this out.

However, looking at your weight alone *can* give you insight into trends over time. If you know your starting weight, it's fairly easy to gauge if you are losing or gaining weight. Some people find that weighing themselves regularly (like once a week) helps them stay on track with their goals because they can see results fairly quickly. Others prefer not paying attention to small fluctuations on the scale and instead use the "jeans test" – i.e. are your jeans/clothes feeling extra tight or extra loose? That might be an indicator of your weight trends. Using the fit of clothes is also very helpful for athletes, as you may be increasing your proportion of lean mass and decreasing fat mass. This can mean you weigh the same amount but your clothes fit better and you have a more toned physique.

Body Fat

Your body is a mixture of bone, water, muscle, organs, and fat. Assessing what percent of your body is fat mass is another way of determining if you're at a healthy weight.

Percent body fat can be measured in a few different ways. The first is called bioelectrical impedance (BIA) – this is the kind that is used when you step on a scale or hold a device that measures body fat. The device sends an electrical signal through your body and determines how quickly it travels, which is related to your body composition. Another way is to have a trainer or doctor use skinfold calipers to measure different areas of your body and put together an average percent body fat. If you have your body fat measured with either of these methods, remember that there is always a margin of error. BIA is very sensitive to hydration, and skinfold caliper accuracy depends heavily on the skill of the person conducting the analysis. There are other methods, like the BodPod or DEXA, which are much more accurate but are typically quite expensive and used mainly in research.

Once you have your body fat measured, you can assess it using the American Council on Exercise (ACE) standards below:

Category	Women	Men
Essential fat (the amount we need for good health)	10-14%	2-5%
Athletes	14-20%	6-13%
Fitness	21-24%	14-17%
Average	25-31%	18-24%
Obese	32%+	25%+

Dropping below levels of essential fat can have negative healthy consequences, as can having fat levels in the obese range.

Making changes to your weight

If using these methods like BMI or body fat analysis shows you are in a healthy range, and these numbers are staying stable – you're likely eating the right amount for your body. However, if you are unhappy with your current weight and/or you fall in an unhealthy weight range, here are some tips you can use to work towards a weight gain or loss goal.

If you want to gain weight…
If you're underweight and you'd like to gain weight, you'll need to eat more calories than you're currently eating or reduce the amount of exercise you're doing. I won't spend too much time on this section because I think most athletes are either looking to lose weight or are content about where the scale currently stands. But I do have a few tips for those of you looking to gain!

The easiest way to gain weight is by adding nutrient-rich, high calorie items to your meal plan. Here are some examples of calorie dense foods that still provide lots of nutrition:
- Nuts and nut butters
- Dried fruit, like dried mangos, cherries, apples, raisins, and any others available
- Higher calorie vegetables – corn, potatoes, sweet potatoes
- Higher calorie fruits – bananas, avocado, figs
- Smoothies – fruits blended with yogurt/milk/other add-ins like flax, chia seeds, coconut, etc.
- Hummus on pita bread
- Pasta tossed with olive oil & parmesan cheese
- Drinks like Carnation Instant Breakfast
- Snack ideas: pudding, cheese, hardboiled eggs
- Consider adding dry milk powder to foods like macaroni & cheese or soups

Other tips:

1) Include frequent snacks and meals throughout the day to increase your calorie intake.

2) Eat higher calorie foods first at a meal, followed by lower calorie foods/drinks.

3) Even though full fat milk and cheeses are higher in calories compared to their lower-fat counterparts, they also contain saturated fat – too much of which is not healthy for us. They can still be helpful tools in increasing calorie intake, but be mindful of the amounts being used and try to vary those tools with other items listed.

My favorite recommendation for athletes looking to gain weight is to add a peanut butter and banana sandwich as a snack. If you use 2 tablespoons of peanut butter, a medium banana, and two slices of whole wheat bread – you're looking at an extra 450 to 500 calories added to your day (plus a dose of healthy fats, potassium, and fiber).

If you want to lose weight…
If you're overweight and would like to lose weight, but you haven't seen the scale drop yet, you need to drop the number of calories you're eating and/or increase the number of calories you burn through exercise.

If you are worried that your body weight is too high and is negatively impacting your training, the best time to address weight management is in the off-season or early in your training regimen. It can be quite difficult to drop those pounds in the midst of a heavy training load.

Many people question this. I often hear, "But you're burning so many calories with training, it should be easy to lose weight!" Yes, you do burn a lot of calories in your workouts. But here are some reasons why you may not be as successful losing weight during the peak of training:

1) Even though long training sessions burn tons of calories, they also stimulate your appetite. You may feel very hungry later in the day and overcompensate with food intake.

2) Many people feel tired later in the day when they are putting their all into long training sessions. This can lead to a relatively sedentary day (or days!) after a long session. For example, picture doing a two hour run in the morning and then vegging out on the couch the rest of the day. You burn a lot of calories during the run, but you burn significantly less the rest of the day.

3) In order to properly fuel your muscles for your training sessions, you have to eat the right foods and the right amount. You may be surprised initially at the amount of carbohydrates required to fuel your muscles. If you cut your food intake too low, you won't be providing your muscles with that essential energy. The result? Your workouts feel hard, you feel fatigued early, and you don't recover as well.

If you decide that weight loss is a priority for you, you'll need to create a caloric deficit. Again, this should preferably be done in the off-season or early in your training schedule, as a caloric deficit in peak training season will compromise performance.

You want to consume just a little less than what your body burns each day. To be able to maintain your level of activity, do not drop too low. Once you have an idea of how many calories your body needs each day (using either the calculations discussed earlier, by estimating how much you are taking in using a food log, or by metabolic rate assessment), consider reducing that by 10 to 20 percent of your current needs, or around 500 calories each day – whichever is less.

For example, let's say your body currently needs about 2200 calories. You'd calculate 20 percent of this and find that equals 440 calories. You wouldn't want to cut more than that many calories each day. A larger drop would likely reduce energy levels and workout performance.

A healthy rate of weight loss is only approximately a ½ pound to 2 pounds per week – we're not striving for *Biggest Loser* numbers here. If you're losing at a rate higher than this, you are likely sacrificing your training by not giving your body enough calories.

Food records for athletes

Food records can be an excellent tool for athletes, especially if you are trying to lose or gain weight. Research shows that people who keep food journals are more likely to be successful in achieving their weight goals (Kong et al, 2012). This tool can help you identify problem areas in your diet, emotional eating issues, training regimens that increase your hunger, and can help you stay accountable to your goals. As an athlete, you can also use it to assess how well you are meeting your carbohydrate and protein needs each day, as well as the effectiveness of your pre-, during-, and post-exercise fueling.

You don't need much to get started, just a notebook that fits in your bag. You can also use a pre-printed form on paper, an online website, or an app for your smartphone. Some of the websites my clients have had success with include:
- SuperTracker - www.choosemyplate.gov/supertracker-tools/supertracker.html
- MyFitnessPal - www.myfitnesspal.com
- Fit Day - www.fitday.com/
- Lose It - www.loseit.com

Tips on keeping a food record
- Include the time of the day and whether you consider those foods a meal or snack.
- Be sure to note portion sizes. Don't just say that you had pasta. How much pasta did you have? One cup? One small bowl? A large bowl? Did you go back for seconds?
- Make notes about your training on your food log. For example, did you eat those two bowls of cereal after a ride? Be sure to jot that down so you know. This can help you identify whether you're eating appropriate pre-exercise meals, during-exercise fueling choices, and recovery foods.

- Write down what you eat while you are eating or directly after. Don't get into the habit of saying, "I'll write this down tonight." You'll most likely forget something, or inaccurately estimate how much you had. Fill it out as you eat throughout the day.
- Avoid "forgotten bites." Did you grab a few M&Ms from the candy bowl at work? Pick up a coffee with cream on your way home from work? Eat a few bites that were leftover on your kids' plates? Make sure you write down everything that you eat or drink.
- It is often helpful to include your mood or events that are going on at the time you are eating. This helps you identify emotional eating patterns, like if you often reach for sweets when you're upset or salty chips when you're bored. It can also identify environmental triggers, like if you eat high calorie entrées when dining out with friends.

Benefits of a food record
- You can easily see your habits. This includes what you are eating, when you eat it, and where your habits could be better. You may find that you make poor choices in certain places, like the work vending machine or certain restaurants. Or maybe you realize that you are waking up late and not leaving yourself enough time to eat breakfast before your morning runs, and that leaves you feeling tired during the run and later on.
- Helps you stick to your meal plan better. If you are underweight and striving to gain weight by eating calorie/nutrient rich snacks, having a food journal can keep you accountable to this goal because you know you'll need to write down what you're eating. Along the same lines, if you are trying to lose weight, you'll be able to see some areas where you could cut calories.

- Track progress. If you keep a food record over time, you can see how your new habits and dietary changes take shape and become second nature.
- For athletes, you can track the changes needed from off-season to pre-season to competition. For example, maybe you notice that in off-season you started to gain weight eating at a certain calorie level, so you had to drop down a bit. Next off-season, you now know to make those changes more quickly.

In the appendix of this book, you'll find a sample food record that you can use to record your own meals. On the next page, you'll find a sample record that shows how you might write down items, portions, and other notes.

Sample Food Record:

Time of day	Meal, snack, or drink. Include the type of food, any preparation details (i.e. fried vs. baked), and portion size (1/2 cup of rice; 10 strawberries; etc).	-Notes about how you felt before eating (hungry, bored, tired...) -Notes about training (i.e. "before bike ride" or "during run"
7AM	Meal: 1 cup of Cheerios with ½ cup skim milk; Medium banana Tall glass of water	Hungry/tired, woke up at 6AM
9AM	Snack - About 20 M&Ms	Candy jar was out at work – I have a hard time passing by.
10:30AM	Snack - 10 carrots with ¼ cup hummus	Hungry
12PM	Fuel during exercise - 16 ounces of Gatorade	Drank during 8 mile lunchtime run
1:30PM	Meal: 6 inch turkey sub on whole wheat bread with 4 ounces turkey, 2 slices cheese, ¼ cup spinach, ¼ cup tomatoes, 2 tbsp mustard Apple 20 ounce Diet coke	Hungry after my run but stomach was a little upset – ate slow but still feeling not great after
5PM	Snacks: 1 margarita 10 nachos topped with cheddar cheese, tomatoes, 2 tbsp sour cream	Happy hour with coworkers
7PM	Meal: 1 cup whole wheat pasta tossed with 1 cup roasted vegetables, 5 ounces grilled chicken, and ½ cup marinara sauce	Tired

Mindful Eating

Another tool in the weight loss arsenal is practicing mindful eating. This strategy is probably best practiced first in the off-season. The basic premise of mindful eating is eating when hungry, stopping when satisfied. Sounds simple, right? Unfortunately, many people don't pay attention to these internal hunger signals and use environmental triggers and emotional cues as signals to eat. Here are some tips to practice mindful eating:

Eat when hungry, stop when satisfied. Your body needs food to function, and it's important to honor that. Along the same lines, we don't want to eat to the point of being overly stuffed (picture the post-Thanksgiving unbuttoning of the pants). Instead, when you feel comfortably satisfied, go ahead and stop.

Fuel your body with healthy choices, most of the time. Eating unhealthy, overly processed foods is probably going to make you feel tired and sluggish. Choose foods for your body that are going to supply you with energy and make you feel good. That being said, no one's diet is 100 percent perfect. You can indulge in some unhealthy choices occasionally without feeling guilty.

Evaluate emotions. This is actually quite hard if you're not used to doing it. If you feel hungry, evaluate whether you are physically hungry or whether it is coming from a mental need: Are you bored? Are you upset? Food won't fix any of these. It may provide a temporary level of satisfaction, but it won't fix the underlying problem.

Take a break for meals. Put down the cell phone, close the computer, turn off the television, and sit down. Focus on your meal. With each bite, take satisfaction in the delicious tastes you have put on your plate. Eat slowly and mindfully, enjoying your meal until you feel satisfied.

Avoiding Fad Diets

One piece of advice that I can't stress enough when you are training for a long road race or a triathlon and are trying to lose weight: do not (I repeat, do not) start some random fad diet. Fad diets are those crazy diet plans that promise you unattainable results in short periods of time. Almost all fad diets are unhealthy, particularly for athletes who have specific nutrient needs. If you are looking at a new diet or meal plan while training and any of the statements below are part of that program, you should probably skip right on over it. As I mentioned above, the best way to work towards weight loss as an endurance athlete is to try to do so in the off season and utilize small caloric deficits.

Here are some fad diet red flags to watch out for…

Red Flag #1: "Drink only cayenne pepper and lemon juice!"
Our bodies need a proper balance of all nutrients and food groups – that's what makes it run properly. And this is even more important when you are getting your body ready for a race! If a diet is asking you to cut out entire groups of foods or nutrients, it's likely not a healthy choice. Not to mention many diets that cut out excessive numbers of foods are likely to be too low in calories, which can slow down your metabolism and sabotage your long term weight loss and training efforts.

Red Flag #2: "You'll lose 15 pounds in five days!"
Don't trust a program that makes promises for excessive amounts of weight loss in a short period of time. Remember, a healthy rate of weight loss is only about a half pound to two pounds per week. Any diet or program that promises more than that rate of weight loss is not healthy and probably unrealistic in its promises.

Red Flag #3: "Try our magical supplement blend!"
Any diet regimen that promotes some mysterious combination of
supplements to help you lose weight is not a healthy option.
Supplements don't create weight loss; eating properly and
exercising do. Many supplements are not backed by evidence-
based research, and some can actually have harmful side effects
depending on your health history. That being said, there are some
supplements that could be useful and beneficial for an athlete if
they are not getting those nutrients in their diet, but even these
won't help you lose weight. For example, if an athlete isn't getting
enough Vitamin D in their diet, they may want to take a
supplement to support bone health. However, this won't help that
person lose weight, and we should always try to meet our needs
through food for any nutrient before reaching for a pill.

Red Flag #4: "It's a weight loss breakthrough!"
When you're reading about the diet plan, does it say it's a
breakthrough? An ancient discovery? A secret to the celebrities?
Miraculous cure-all? Any of these are big indicators that it's a diet
based on "junk science" – aka there is no basis or evidence.

Red Flag #5: "Developed by our own nutrition coach!"
This one could be a legitimate program, but you'll need to do some
detective work. Did you know that anyone can legally call
themselves a "nutritionist" or "nutrition coach" without any actual
training or credentials? Double check to make sure that the
program is developed by a Registered Dietitian, or a nutritionist
like a CCN that has a strong educational background. There are
quite a few short online programs labeling graduates as
"nutritionists." While these individuals may good at promoting
nutrition basics, they're (almost always) not specialized enough to
give recommendations for endurance athletes.

Don't fall for silly fad diet ploys. Eating healthy and exercising are the lifelong tools for maintaining a healthy weight and optimizing performance!

TL;DR Tips on Energy Needs and Weight Management

- You can estimate your energy needs using calculations, food logs, or metabolic rate assessment.
- The more you train, the higher your calorie needs.
- The best time to try to lose weight is in the off-season or early in training.
- To lose weight, cut around 10-20% of your daily calorie needs, or approximately 250 to 500 calories per day – whichever range is less – in order to minimize the effect on training.
- Tools like food records can help you work towards weight loss or weight gain goals.

Carbohydrates: Essential Fuel

Carbohydrates: Essential Fuel

Carbohydrates have gotten a bad reputation over the last decade. Popular diets like South Beach, Atkins, and Paleo have led much of the general public to believe that carbohydrates are the source of unsightly bulges and belly fat. Not all carbohydrates are bad for us, though. It is actually essential that athletes consume a diet rich in healthy sources of carbohydrates in order to fuel their muscles properly.

What are carbohydrates exactly?

At its simplest, a carbohydrate is either a single sugar molecule or a combination of such. We can separate carbohydrates into two groups: simple sugars and complex carbohydrates. Simple sugars include individual sugar molecules called monosaccharides (like glucose and fructose) or a combination of two sugar molecules, which is called a disaccharide. An example of a disaccharide would be sucrose – the scientific name for table sugar – which is made up of an equal ratio of glucose and fructose. Complex carbohydrates are chains of sugar molecules that form starches and fiber.

Dietary fiber is a plant component that falls under the category of a complex carbohydrate but is actually indigestible by our gastrointestinal system. There are two different types of dietary fiber: soluble and insoluble. Soluble fiber forms a gel-like substance inside our digestive system, which helps to slow gastrointestinal transit time as well as bind cholesterol, decreasing its absorption. Ever see a box of *Cherrios* with the words "part of a heart-healthy diet" or "may lower cholesterol"? That's because oats – the primary ingredient in Cheerios – contain a good amount of soluble fiber. Soluble fiber can also help your body slow the absorption of sugars, so when you eat a food rich in it you doesn't experience as rapid an increase in blood sugar compared to foods without fiber. Soluble fiber is found in foods like oats, barley, legumes, citrus fruit, apples, and strawberries.

The second type of fiber is called insoluble fiber. Insoluble fiber increases the ability of waste material to hold water and "bulks up" stool. When you hear that fiber "helps keep you regular," this is what people are talking about. Insoluble fiber comes from sources like whole grains, vegetables, and many fruits.

This Institute of Medicine recommends male adults get a total of 38 grams of fiber each day and female adults get a total of 25 grams per day, coming from both soluble and insoluble types.

Which carbohydrates are healthiest?
Many people will claim that complex carbohydrates are preferable to simple carbohydrates. However, this is an oversimplification. For example, white bread is comprised of mostly complex carbohydrates, while grapes are mostly simple sugars. I would argue that in most (if not all) cases, the grapes are going to be the better choice because they're rich in vitamins and phytochemicals.

Rather than worrying about the specific type of carbohydrate, aim to make choices that are rich in many nutrients and support an overall healthy lifestyle. This includes fruits, vegetables, legumes (beans & lentils), whole grains, and low fat dairy.

But aren't carbohydrates fattening? Don't they cause health problems?
The media sometimes claims that carbohydrates are responsible for the increasing rates of overweight/obesity and metabolic health problems. But this message is being taken out of context. They fail to distinguish the different sources of carbohydrates and nutrient density of foods. It's true that excessive *refined* carbohydrates are associated with increased risk of health problems. These are products like donuts, cookies, white bread, etc. These often create a blood sugar spike and have little other nutritional value.

However, carbohydrates from sources like whole grains and fruits/vegetables are perfectly healthy and provide us with many other nutrients. These foods contain a higher fiber content compared to refined grain products, which means that the carbohydrates are broken down and released more slowly in your body. This translates to less of a spike in blood sugar and a more controlled, sustained release of energy throughout the day.

It's also important to keep in mind portion sizes when it comes to carbohydrates, even if they're a whole grain. Many people pile on three to four times the recommended portions when creating meals. The number of portions you should eat at a given time depends on your metabolic rate and physical activity level. A male athlete training for an ultra-marathon, for example, will likely need several portions of carbohydrate-rich foods at a given meal. On the other hand, a female training recreationally a few days a week for a sprint triathlon will likely only need a standard serving or slightly more.

Carbohydrate Recommendations for Athletes

During your training season for endurance sports, it's important that your diet contains adequate amounts of these healthy carbohydrates. Why? Because carbohydrates are your brain's main source of energy *and* they are stored in your muscles to use as a fuel source during exercise!

You'll read about "glycogen" many times in this book. For those of you who are unfamiliar with this term, glycogen refers to carbohydrate that is stored in your muscles and used for energy. In intense exercise, carbohydrates are your body's primary source of energy. In lower intensity exercise, both stored fat and stored carbohydrates are involved as energy sources. Because it is physically impossible to only use fat as energy, we must eat a training diet with healthy sources of carbohydrates in order to provide our muscles with that glycogen for energy.

How much carbohydrate do I need each day?

Daily carbohydrate needs for athletes are based on your training schedule and weight. This makes sense, because if you are heavier and have a greater amount of muscle mass, you'll need a greater amount of carbohydrate to supply energy to that muscle. In general, healthy sources of carbohydrates should make up about 50 to 65 percent of your daily caloric intake during training. You can estimate your carbohydrate needs using the guidelines below. Each recommended intake range is given as grams of carbohydrate per kilogram of body weight.

Training Category	Hours of Training Daily	Recommended Carbohydrate Intake
Very light training	<1 hour of low intensity training daily or 1 hour of low intensity training some days	3-5 grams/kg
Light to moderate training	1 to 1.5 hours per day	5-7 grams/kg
Moderate to heavy training and high intensity training	1 to 3 hours per day	6-10 grams/kg
Heavy training and high intensity training; ultra-endurance training	>3 to 5 hours per day	8-12 grams/kg

*Developed using AND (2013); ADA & ACSM (2009); IOC (2004)

You may notice that there's a little overlap in some of the categories. That is due to differences in intensity that may occur among training plans. For example, someone working out one and a half hours at a very intense level each day might go in the 'moderate to heavy' category while someone working out for one and a half hours at a less intense level might go in the 'light to moderate' category.

As an example, let's say we have a 150 pound female athlete training to achieve a personal best in a half marathon. She works out moderately for one hour most days, and little longer (two hours) on two days during the week. Based on this, we might say she needs about 6 grams of carbohydrate/kg. We would calculate this as follows:

- 150 pounds / 2.2 pounds per kilogram = 68.2 kg
- 68.2 kg x 6 g carbohydrate/kg = 409 grams of carbohydrate everyday

Unfortunately, I can't give you a calculation for *exactly* how many grams of carbohydrates you need in your everyday diet during training to optimize performance. No such calculation exists. But you can use these ranges to make an educated guess and see how your body feels when eating at that level. If you are feeling tired and exhausted often, or experiencing slow recovery, that may be a sign that you need to bump up your carbohydrate intake a bit. If you are gaining weight and feeling bloated after every meal, it may be a sign you need to cut down (though these factors could also relate to overeating another macronutrient like fat).

You can work one-on-one with a dietitian who can review your training schedule, typical intake, and any health conditions and help you estimate the right amounts for you. Be aware that certain medical conditions (specifically diabetes and metabolic syndrome) may affect the amount of carbohydrate and timing of carbohydrate for training.

Training season vs. off-season
The recommendations presented are specific to athletes in training. Those who aren't doing any training should aim for a minimum of 130 grams of carbohydrate per day to support health (Institute of Medicine, 2010). If you're a 70 kilogram person (154 pounds), that's

only about 2 grams of carbohydrate per kilogram, which is much less than most of the ranges listed in our chart. Of course, that's the minimum recommendation, and you can certainly go over that amount in a healthy off-season meal plan – but you just want to be careful about overdoing it.

Overeating carbohydrates when your body doesn't need them can lead to weight gain (if this puts you into a positive caloric balance) and can also lead to poor metabolic outcomes (like altered cholesterol levels) if it's coming from refined sources.

What does this mean? You should adjust your diet during the off-season and during any periods where you are doing less (or no) endurance exercise. For example, if in the winter you cut back on training and are more of a casual gym-goer, you shouldn't be eating the same amount of carbohydrate (or overall calories) that you did during your peak season. Along the same lines, at the height of half-ironman training, you will need considerably more carbohydrate compared to an off-season plan that includes a few short runs and hour long rides on the trainer.

What types of carbohydrates should I be eating to support my training?
While endurance athletes often need more carbohydrates in their diet compared to non-athletes, that doesn't give us free range to eat massive piles of refined grains like white pasta or cake. In fact, eating too many refined carbohydrates can lead to blood sugar and insulin spikes, as well as elevated triglyceride levels (which increases the risk of heart disease). Instead, make the majority of your carb-rich food choices fruits, vegetables, whole grains, legumes, and dairy products, as these will help you meet your carbohydrate needs in a nutrient rich way. Take a look at the next section where we explore nutrition highlights and healthy ideas related to each of these food categories.

TL;DR Tips on Carbohydrate Intake:

- Healthy sources of carbohydrate are not fattening, and are essential to fueling your muscles.
- Carbohydrate recommendations vary based on your weight and training regimen, and should make up a significant (approximately 50-65 percent) portion of your caloric intake.
- Whole grains, fruits, vegetables, legumes, and dairy are all healthy choices that can help you meet your carbohydrate needs.
- You may need to reduce your caloric intake (and thus carbohydrate intake) in the off-season when training volume decreases to support weight management.

Whole Grains

Grains get a bad reputation. People claim they're "unhealthy" or our bodies aren't meant to eat them (see the appendix section on "Paleo" for more information about why this isn't true), and they're often the first thing people cut out when they start dieting. But grains have an essential spot in an athlete's diet because they are often a rich source of carbohydrates and other nutrients. The key when choosing grains is to select **whole** grains.

Here's the deal on whole grains – they contain all three parts of the grain kernel. This includes the:
- *Bran* – This outer layer surrounds the grain and protects it. It provides fiber, B-vitamins, and minerals.
- *Germ* – This is where a lot of nutrients are stored, including antioxidants, Vitamin E, B-vitamins, and healthy fats.
- *Endosperm* – This is the largest part of the grain kernel and contains carbohydrates as well as protein.

Because all the parts of the grain kernel are used in whole grains, we're given an extra boost of fiber that's essential for digestion, blood sugar regulation, and heart health. A refined grain product is typically only made from the endosperm portion – so it provides carbohydrates, but lacks a lot of other nutrients. Some of these lost nutrients are added back in during processing (through enrichment and fortification) but *not* to the same nutritional profile of the original whole grain.

So how do you spot the whole grains? It (unfortunately) isn't as simple as you might think! There are tons of breads or cereals out there that look like they should be whole grain – they're brown in color – and some even say "wheat bread" or "multigrain cereal" in the name of the product. But to truly identify if you're eating a whole grain, you'll need to flip the package over and take a look at the ingredient list. The very first ingredient should say "whole wheat," "whole grain oat flour," "brown rice," or a similar term (for other types of grains) indicating it is the unrefined form. If you see "enriched wheat flour" as the first ingredient, that's just another term for white flour, aka a refined grain product. If it's a multigrain product, look at the different types of grain in the label to see if they are all whole grains.

Sometimes people look at the nutrition facts to check the amount of fiber and purchase products based on this, assuming it's a whole grain because of the high fiber content. This can be deceiving, though, since manufacturers have jumped on the fiber bandwagon and have been adding isolated fibers to foods. These boost the fiber in refined products, making them seem like a healthier choice when in reality they are still not a whole grain. In addition, scientists are not sure if these isolated fibers have the same impact as regular fiber on your body. Your best bet is to read the ingredients and select items that are truly a whole grain.

Let's look at some great examples of carbohydrate-rich whole grains that you can include in your everyday training diet. Keep in mind that the "nutrition highlights" for each item are not the complete nutrition facts panel, but rather some key points.

Brown Rice

If you've been using white rice in your cooking, it's time to change it up to brown rice. These days, it's easy to find many varieties of brown rice at the store, and there is even instant brown rice now available. For busy athletes, instant brown rice can be a life-saver, allowing you to make quick healthy meals at home in just a few minutes.

Nutrition highlights
One cup of brown rice clocks in at 218 calories and provides 46 grams of carbohydrate. It's also got 5 grams of protein, a variety of B vitamins, and about 20 percent of your daily magnesium needs.

Healthy ideas

No time to make a big dinner? Instant brown rice to the rescue!
Check out these three ideas for quick and healthy meals:

1) Cook instant brown rice. Add a can of drained black beans, a can of tomatoes with green chiles, and a chopped avocado. If desired, top with a little shredded cheddar cheese. Dinner is served in 10 minutes flat!

2) Create a stir fry with your favorite veggies and serve over brown rice. I love snap peas, bell peppers, and mushrooms for my stir fries. Add chicken, tofu, or lean beef for a source of protein.

3) Brush chicken with a marinade and bake in the oven. Once cooked, combine with instant brown rice and frozen vegetables that you've heated up.

Qunioa

Quinoa (pronounced keen-wa) is a delicious alternative to rice, pasta, and other grains. It has a mild, nutty flavor. Though it is generally referred to as a whole grain (and we're including it this section for that purpose), technically it's an edible seed. Quinoa is packed with nutrition and can be used in a variety of ways, making it a great alternative for athletes who need a change from pasta and rice.

Nutrition highlights

One cup of cooked quinoa contains 222 calories, 39 grams of carbohydrate, and 8 grams of protein – the highest protein content of all the grains. It's also got 5 grams of fiber to support healthy digestion and 30 percent of your daily magnesium needs. Plus, you'll find 15 percent of your daily iron needs, which is very important to athletes as iron is involved in transporting oxygen to your cells.

Quick tip
Quinoa is relatively simple and quick to make. Rinse before using it, and then add to a pot and use a 2:1 liquid to quinoa ratio. Simmer for about 15 minutes, fluff with a fork, and enjoy!

Healthy ideas
Quinoa can be used in many different ways – most easily as a substitute for rice in just about any dish, from casseroles to burritos to a simple dish with beans. But you can also use quinoa as a breakfast option! Make a batch of quinoa ahead of time and store it in the fridge, then warm it up and mix with milk, fruit, nuts, and/or spices (similar to the way you'd prepare oatmeal).

Barley

Barley, often thought of only for its use in beer and baby cereals, is making a major comeback as a mainstream grain. And for good reason – it's quite inexpensive, incredibly nutritious, and can be used in a variety of dishes.

Nutrition highlights
One cup of cooked pearl barley contains 193 calories, 44 grams of carbohydrate, and 6 grams of fiber. You'll also find 4 grams of protein, 12 percent of your daily iron needs, and 19 percent of your daily selenium needs (a mineral involved in antioxidant reactions).

Types of barley
Pearl barley is the most widely available product. It has been polished to remove the inedible hull layer, as well as part of the (edible) bran layer. Pearled barley is technically not considered a whole grain because part of the bran layer is removed. However, barley is unique in that its fiber and vitamin/mineral content are distributed more evenly throughout the different parts of the grain kernel (as opposed to other grains where it's concentrated only in one part). Because of this, pearled barley still maintains a very high fiber and micronutrient content. Whole grain barley is similar to

pearled barley in that its hull layer has been removed, but whole grain barley still contains the entire bran layer. This product is sometimes referred to as hulled or hulless barley, but it can be more difficult to find in stores.

Healthy ideas
If you're struggling with ways to use barley, consider these simple options:
- Add barley to any soup recipe that is going to cook for a while. Think beef and barley soups or vegetable soups!
- Make stuffed bell peppers, but substitute barley for the rice.
- Create a grain salad using cooked barley, chopped peaches, tomatoes, cucumbers, and chickpeas. Top with a light vinaigrette using two parts cider vinegar and one part oil.
- Try barley for breakfast. You can use this as a hot cereal dish similar to oatmeal & quinoa. Add chopped fresh or dried fruit, cinnamon, coconut, or nuts for variety.

Whole Wheat
Wheat makes up a large portion of many people's grain choices, as it's found in pastas, breads, cereals, and more. The nutrition facts for products made from whole wheat obviously vary based on what the food is, what other ingredients are in it, and how it is prepared.

Healthy ideas
Because whole wheat products are widely available, I don't doubt that you already know many ways to utilize these choices, but just in case, here are a few ideas:
- Create whole wheat pancakes or waffles and then top with fruit.
- Always hungry for a snack in the mid-afternoon slump? Consider a quick bowl of whole wheat cereal with a ½ cup of skim milk (or a milk substitute).
- Top a slice of whole wheat toast with peanut butter.

- Substitute whole wheat bread for the white bread on your sandwich.
- Utilize whole wheat tortillas for wraps or burritos.
- Try a whole wheat pasta salad: combine cooked pasta with chopped tomatoes, bell peppers, broccoli, and cheddar cheese. When you're ready to eat it, top with a little Italian dressing.

Oats

Oats are inexpensive, minimally processed, and incredibly healthy. They're easy to incorporate in daily breakfasts and can be added to a variety of other meals/snacks.

Nutrition highlights

A quarter cup of dry steel cut oats or ½ cup of dry rolled oats contains 150 calories and 27 grams of carbohydrate. It contains 4 grams of fiber and 5 grams of protein. Plus, you'll get 10 percent or more of your daily needs for iron, zinc, magnesium, or selenium.

Quick tip

Steel cut oats are the most natural form and are slightly less processed. The way that they're cut makes them more densely concentrated so their portion size is smaller. They also have a bit of a chewier texture. Regular rolled oats are still a wonderful choice though, and are almost equal in nutritional value. Because they're steamed and rolled out into flakes, though, they're less dense and the dry serving size is larger. The more highly processed individual packets of instant oatmeal often have a lot of added sugar, but can be a good choice if you need something quick and on-the-go. However, you can make your healthier own grab-and-go packets by portioning out oats from the inexpensive containers of steel cut or rolled oats. Then add your own fruits, spices, nuts, etc.

Healthy ideas

- Include oatmeal as a regular part of your breakfast. Cook steel cut or rolled oats according to package directions, and then add in some of your other favorite items. For example, you could try oatmeal with sliced peaches, pecans, and a teaspoon of maple syrup. Or try oatmeal with a sliced apple, cinnamon, and a teaspoon of brown sugar.
- Try overnight oats. You'll mix oats, yogurt, and fruit (and sometimes milk) in a jar and leave it in the fridge overnight. The next morning, you have a cold ready-to-go breakfast.
- Add oats to your favorite baked goods, like pancakes or quick breads. Or try your hand at making homemade granola bars.
- Place oats in a food processor and pulse, then use these as a substitute for breadcrumbs to coat chicken and fish. Or use oats in a burger or meatloaf recipe that calls for breadcrumbs.

Grain considerations before a long training session or race

I'll delve deeply into pre-exercise nutrition later in the book, but I think this is worth touching on here. Before a very long training session or race, sometimes you may want to choose (and this usually surprises people) refined grains. That's right, sometimes refined grains are appropriate – and before you start questioning everything I've told you up until this point, here's the reason why. We all know that wheat bread and brown rice are healthier than white bread and white rice in our everyday diet. However, in the meal directly before a *long* training session or race, the extra fiber in the whole grains may cause you to feel full and may stir up some gastrointestinal issues. This is particularly true if you're eating close to the race (within an hour or so). If you're like me, I know you probably want to avoid the dreaded "runner's trots" out on the course!

Now, some people have a 'regular' digestive pattern. These individuals may prefer to eat whole grains that morning because they know that every morning after they eat they'll use the bathroom and feel cleared out and comfortable. But if your body doesn't work like that, you may feel better off sticking to some of the lower-fiber options for breakfast before a long run/ride/race. Experiment with what works for you, and if you can eat whole grains without any problems during exercise, they're certainly the better option for overall health.

TL;DR Tips on Whole Grains

- Whole grains contain more fiber, vitamins, and minerals compared to refined grains.
- Brown rice, quinoa, barley, oats, and whole wheat products are all whole grains rich in carbohydrate that can be incorporated into an endurance athlete's diet.
- Some athletes prefer to eat refined grains in a meal before a long workout/race, since the extra fiber in whole grains may stir up digestive trouble. This is highly individualized.

Fruits

Aside from whole grains, fruits are another food group that is rich in carbohydrates. Athletes should aim for a minimum of two cups of fruit each day, but many need more. While just about every fruit out there is a good source of carbohydrate and can support your training diet, I wanted to highlight a few of my personal favorites that are superstars for athletes.

Apples
Often overlooked because they're so commonplace, apples definitely deserve a spot in your fruit bowl. They're nutritious, delicious, and quite inexpensive. Plus, one medium apple counts as 1 cup of fruit, helping you get on your way towards meet your daily needs.

Nutrition highlights
A medium sized apple contains 95 calories and 25 grams of carbohydrate. You'll also get 4 grams of fiber and 14 percent of the daily value for Vitamin C. Plus, apples contain quercetin, an antioxidant which is thought to have anti-inflammatory properties and may also slightly increase endurance exercise performance (Kressler et al, 2011).

Healthy ideas
- Add chopped apples to your favorite mac and cheese recipe. It sounds odd, but the salty/sweet combo is delicious.
- Carry apples with you for an easy, portable snack. Eat them with peanut butter, nuts, or a string cheese for a snack that provides healthy carbohydrates, fiber, and protein/healthy fat.
- Craving a sweet dessert? Try baking an apple and topping it with cinnamon, raisins, and/or nuts.
- Create a delicious and filling salad with this easy recipe: Mix 2 cups of salad greens with 3-4 ounces of grilled

chicken, 1 sliced apple, 1/3 cup dried cranberries, ½ ounce pecans and 2 tbsp lite balsamic vinaigrette. Enjoy with hearty whole wheat roll or a baked potato on the side to boost the carbohydrate count for an in-season training meal.

Bananas
As one of the most common fruits used by athletes, bananas are excellent for fueling your exercise.

Nutrition highlights
A large banana contains 121 calories and 31 grams of carbohydrate, including 3.5 grams of fiber. Known for its potassium content, it provides about 485 mg – or 14 percent – of your daily needs. It also provides about 20 percent of the daily value for Vitamin C.

Healthy ideas
- Having a hard time meeting your calorie and carbohydrate needs to fuel performance? Try this snack: spread peanut butter or almond butter over graham crackers, and top with sliced bananas.
- Slice a banana and freeze. Transfer to a food processor or blender and add a dash of milk. Process for a few minutes, until the consistency becomes smooth. Voila! It's banana "ice cream"!
- Leave bananas out too long? Those ones with brown spots are perfect for whipping up a homemade whole wheat banana bread.
- Dip sliced bananas in Greek yogurt and freeze for a cold treat.

Blackberries
Blackberries are a delicious addition to meals and snacks. In the US, blackberry season typically peaks in June or July. You can also find them year-round in the frozen fruit section, and since they're frozen at the peak of freshness, they're just as nutritious as fresh!

49

One cup of blackberries contains 62 calories and 15 grams of carbohydrate, plus a whopping 8 grams of fiber for digestive health. You'll also meet 50 percent of the daily value for Vitamin C and get a hefty dose of anthocyanins, a potent phytochemical with antioxidant properties.

Healthy ideas
- Add blackberries to smoothies. Try a blend of orange juice, plain Greek yogurt, strawberries, blackberries, and mango. You'll end up with a fiber-filled smoothie that packs tons of antioxidants, Vitamin C, and a boost of calcium/protein.
- You can also experiment with making popsicles from those smoothie recipes.
- Heat some blackberries and raspberries in the microwave or on the stovetop until they start to release some of their juices. Pour over whole wheat pancakes or waffles for a great alternative to syrup. This is a particularly good use for frozen berries.
- Use blackberries in recipes that might call for other berries or fruits. For example, in a recipe for apple glazed pork loin, try blackberries instead.
- Add blackberries to cornbread mix before baking.

Blueberries
Blueberries are grown in 35 different states across the US and are harvested from mid-April through October with peak harvests in July.

Nutrition highlights
One cup of blueberries contains 80 calories, 21 grams of carbohydrate, and 4 grams of dietary fiber. You'll also get 24 percent of the daily value for Vitamin C. They're one of the best sources of antioxidants out there, filled with quercetin and anthocyanidins.

- Sprinkle blueberries on top of your cold cereal, oatmeal, whole wheat pancakes, or whole grain waffles.
- Put a new spin on pasta salad. Combine whole wheat pasta with grilled chicken, blueberries, feta cheese, and caramelized onions.
- Create "spa water" by adding blueberries, lemon, and/or cucumbers to a pitcher of ice water.
- Create rainbow fruit kebobs for your next party or barbeque. Use blueberries for the blue portion, and be creative with which fruits you use for the rest of the colors.
- Dip blueberries in yogurt, roll in granola, and freeze. Enjoy as a healthy snack.

Cherries
Cherries are grown in the summer months and have a short growing season. Stay away from the overly processed maraschino cherries (the ones you typically find on top of an ice cream sundae) and stick with sweet and tart varieties of fresh cherries instead.

Nutrition highlights
One cup of sweet cherries contains 87 calories and 22 grams of carbohydrate. That cup packs over 300 mg of potassium, important for heart and muscular health, and 16 percent of your daily Vitamin C requirement. Plus, it contains anthocyanins, a powerful antioxidant phytochemical, as well as melatonin, a compound that may improve sleep quality (Howatson et al, 2012).

Tart vs. sweet
Sweet cherries are the type most easily found in the grocery store. They range in color from golden with hints of red to a deep purple. They may be round or somewhat heart shaped. Tart cherries, on the other hand, are usually a bright red color and have a rounder shape. These may be found at farmers markets or CSA programs, or occasionally at some grocery stores. Tart cherries contain more

antioxidants, melatonin, and quercetin compared to sweet cherries (though sweet cherries are still a healthy choice). Tart cherries also have less sugar, so sometimes people don't like their taste.

Healthy ideas
- Sweet cherries are a great snack, and their thicker flesh tends to hold up well when you toss a bag of cherries in your purse or briefcase for the day.
- Slice the cherries and remove their pits. Combine with orange or tangerine segments, blueberries, and kiwi for a flavorful fruit salad.
- Add dried unsweetened cherries to a homemade trail mix or your morning oatmeal.
- Top a salad with fresh cherries or dried cherries.
- Substitute chopped cherries for blueberries in quick bread or muffin mixes.

Dates
While dates may not be the most beautiful fruit to look at, they are great for athletes due to their rich carbohydrate content. Medjool dates are the largest in size and the sweetest. They are plump and taste great eaten fresh. You may also see deglect noor dates at the supermarket, which are smaller, chewier, and a bit drier.

Nutrition highlights
Three pitted medjool dates contain 200 calories and a whopping 54 grams of natural carbohydrate. There's also 5 grams of dietary fiber, 500 mg of potassium (15 percent of your daily needs), 10 percent of your magnesium needs, and a high amount of polyphenols (a type of antioxidant). About 10 deglect noor dates provide the same nutrition as 3 medjool dates.

Quick tip
Dates have the lowest moisture content of any natural fruit – just 30 percent moisture. They are like nature's own version of dried fruit.

This means they can last longer than other fresh fruits, but you still want to eat them in a reasonable amount of time for optimal flavor. Store them in an airtight container in the fridge for up to several months, or freeze them for longer. Most should also be fine left out at room temperature for several weeks.

Healthy ideas
- Blend chopped dates with nuts in a food processor, and then shape to create your own homemade energy bars.
- Remove the pit from the date and add a little peanut butter for a quick snack comprised of both carbohydrates, healthy fats, and a protein.
- For a sweet and salty combo, wrap dates with prosciutto or ham and sprinkle with a little ground pepper.
- Add chopped dates to your cold cereal, hot oatmeal, or your morning yogurt.
- Create a homemade trail mix with whole grain cereal, chopped deglect noor dates, and nuts.
- Puree Medjool dates with a little warm milk and use it to drizzle over a whole grain waffle.

Grapes
Grapes are one of the most delicious pieces of fruit out there – a true example of "nature's candy." They're also great because they're portable and easy to eat on the go; there's no messy peeling or cutting needed.

Nutrition highlights
One cup of grapes contains 104 calories and 27 grams of carbohydrate, plus 27 percent of the daily value for Vitamin C and 288 mg (8 percent) of your daily potassium needs. Red grapes contain high levels of resveratrol, an antioxidant that may play a role in cancer prevention (AICR, 2011). And while we certainly can't draw conclusions to humans yet, in animal research

resveratrol has been shown to improve endurance exercise performance (Dolinsky et al, 2012).

Healthy ideas
- Freeze the grapes! This is especially useful if you know you won't be able to eat all the fresh ones you bought before they'll go bad. Frozen grapes have a consistency similar to a popsicle, but with so many more nutrients.
- Add chopped grapes to chicken salad or tuna fish for a unique taste on these classic sandwich fillers.
- Slice grapes and put them over whole grain waffles.
- Raisins (dried grapes) make an excellent carbohydrate choice to fuel long bike rides or runs.

Kiwi
Though some people see them as the ugly ducklings of the produce aisle because of their fuzzy brown exterior, kiwis are a top choice for athletes. They're quite inexpensive, running just 20 to 50 cents each, making them an economical option for those of us on a budget. Imported kiwis can be found in supermarkets year round and can be stored in the fridge for 1-2 weeks.

Nutrition highlights
A medium kiwi contains 42 calories and 10 grams of carbohydrate, including 2 grams of dietary fiber. Plus, just one of these tiny fruits has over 100 percent of the daily value for Vitamin C.

Quick tips
- Worried about taking kiwi as a snack because you don't want to carry a peeler? No problem. Just slice the kiwi in half and eat it with a spoon. The skin acts as a miniature bowl.
- A word of warning – if you are allergic to latex, you may also have an allergy to kiwi. Kiwis contain a protein that is

chemically similar to latex and sometimes causes reactions in those who have a latex allergy.

Healthy ideas
- Chop up a kiwi and papaya and add them to your morning oatmeal for a taste from the tropics.
- In the mood for a homemade dessert? Try some cinnamon chips with fruit salsa. Brush whole wheat tortillas with olive oil and sprinkle cinnamon sugar over them. Cut into wedges and bake them in a 350 degree oven for about 10 minutes. Allow to cool while you make the salsa. Mix finely chopped apple, strawberries, kiwi, and raspberries together. Eat with your cinnamon chips. Yum!
- Top grilled fish or pork with a fruit salsa made from kiwi, mango, and red onion.
- Kiwi can be great for marinating meat and actually acts as a tenderizer. Puree kiwi, soy sauce, garlic, and a little oil together and use it to marinate chicken, lamb, or beef.

Mango
Considered the most popular fruit worldwide, mangoes come in several varieties that range in taste from super sweet to slightly spicy.

Nutrition highlights
A large mango contains 202 calories and 50 grams of carbohydrate, including 5 grams of fiber. It packs a powerful nutrition punch, with over 70 percent of your daily Vitamin A requirements and 200 percent of your daily Vitamin C requirements.

Healthy ideas
- Add fresh mangoes to a fruit salad with blueberries, strawberries, and pomegranate.
- Over the summer, try grilling mango & shrimp skewers topped with Caribbean jerk seasoning.

- Puree fresh mango in a blender or food processor with 100 percent orange juice, then freeze with popsicle sticks for a frozen fruit pop.
- Add chopped mango, red onion, and curry powder to a chicken salad recipe for a new take on an old favorite.
- Puree mango with lime juice, jalapeno peppers, and garlic, and use as a glaze for chicken, beef, or fish.
- Liven up your morning oatmeal with fresh mango and shredded coconut.

Oranges

Do you feel like oranges bring you back to your baseball or soccer games as a child? I always remember having orange slices at half time. This fruit is *still* a great choice for athletes, both young and old.

Nutrition highlights

A large orange contains 86 calories and 22 grams of carbohydrate, including 4 grams of fiber. You'll get more than a day's worth of Vitamin C, and 14 percent of your daily folate needs.

Healthy ideas
- Add orange sections to a salad and top with slivered almonds, grilled chicken, and an Asian style vinaigrette dressing.
- Consider adding orange sections to items you might normally use other fruit in, like fruit salads or on top of whole grain waffles.
- Orange juice provides less fiber, so eating an orange is typically better than drinking the juice. However, for many time-pressed athletes, a cup or two of OJ can be a good source of energizing carbohydrate at breakfast or after a long workout.
- Squeeze oranges onto chicken or pork while cooking them for a citrusy boost of flavor.

Peaches

Juicy, sweet peaches are another great choice for athletes, reaching peak season in the summer months.

Nutrition highlights

A large peach contains 68 calories and 17 grams of carbohydrate. You'll get 10 percent of the daily value for Vitamin A, 17 percent of the daily value for Vitamin C, and 285 mg (8 percent) of your daily potassium needs.

Healthy ideas

- Use peaches in grain-based salads like quinoa or barley salads.
- Try one of my favorite breakfasts: Cook one serving of plain oatmeal according to package directions. Add one large or two small sliced peaches, ¼ cup of pecans, and 1 teaspoon of brown sugar. It's delicious and will keep you full throughout the morning.
- Add peaches to your smoothies or yogurt.
- Grill peaches (it caramelizes the sugar – yum!) and top with pecans for a healthy dessert.
- Combine sweet peaches with spicy arugula and a little crumbled blue cheese for a side salad.

Pears

Pears are nutritious, easy to find at pretty much any grocery store, and come in several delicious varieties. The flavor of pears can vary between choices, from Anjou to Bartlett to Bosc.

Nutrition highlights

A medium pear contains 101 calories and 27 grams of carbohydrate, including 6 grams of fiber. Different types of pears contain different antioxidants, so be sure to try a variety. And eat the skins! The skin of many fruits, like pears and apples, are actually concentrated sources of fiber and nutrients.

Healthy ideas
- Make fish tacos and top with a pear-mango salsa.
- "Healthify" your grilled cheese by adding pear slices and arugula in the sandwich.
- Cook an acorn squash, and then stuff with wild rice, chopped pears, cranberries, and walnuts.
- Bake a pear with some cinnamon and nutmeg for a sweet treat after dinner.
- Instead of applesauce, make "pear sauce." There are several crockpot recipes online that are simple and require little cooking knowledge or preparation.

Pineapple

I love the juicy, sweet flavor of pineapple. Plus, it's versatile and can be used in a wide range of dishes from snacks to entrées to desserts.

Nutrition highlights
One cup of chopped raw pineapple contains 82 calories and 22 grams of carbohydrate. It packs over a day's worth of Vitamin C, as well as bromelain, a digestive enzyme. Some researchers postulate that bromelain may also help reduce inflammation in the body (Hale et al, 2010). On an interesting note, this enzyme is the reason why pineapple is such a good meat tenderizer.

Healthy ideas
- Make a stir fry by sautéing broccoli, mushrooms, onions, bell pepper, and pineapple. Serve over brown rice. Add chicken or tofu for extra protein.
- Sprinkle raw chicken with an Italian dried herb blend, then bake. Chop pineapple and red onion and use this "salsa" to top your chicken. Serve with a baked sweet potato and you've got a delicious balanced meal.
- Hawaiian pizza can be healthy, especially if you make it at home! Top a whole wheat pizza crust with tomato sauce,

part skim mozzarella cheese, pineapple, and a few pieces of chopped lower sodium ham. Add some extra veggies like mushrooms or peppers.
- Want a delicious dessert that also provides a serving of fruit, plus some calcium and protein? Grill pineapple for a few minutes (or spray a pan with cooking spray and sauté the pineapple until the sugar starts to caramelize a bit). Mix with a ½ cup low fat Greek frozen yogurt and shredded coconut.

Pomegranate

Pomegranates are limited by seasonality, but are definitely a winner for runners and triathletes when they're available. Fresh whole ones can be found in the winter months, and you can also find pomegranate juices in the store throughout the year. And no, you don't have to spit out the seeds – they are completely edible and a great source of fiber!

Nutrition highlights

A pomegranate contains 235 calories and 53 grams of carbohydrate. If you eat the seeds, you'll get 11 grams of fiber. Pomegranate is a great source of Vitamin C and potassium, providing about 50 percent and 20 percent of your daily needs, respectively. It's also got high levels of antioxidants – particularly anthocyanins – that promote health.

Quick tip

The easiest and most hassle-free way to open a pomegranate is to cut it and break it in half, then place the fruit in a bowl of water to remove the arils (seeds). As you remove the arils, they will sink to the bottom of the water while the other inedible white part of the flesh floats to the top. No stained clothes!

Healthy ideas

- Sprinkle pomegranate seeds over your favorite fruit salad or your favorite regular salad – they add a burst of flavor and crunch.
- Pomegranate actually pairs quite well with chicken, turkey and pork when made into a glaze or topping.
- Getting bored with regular water? Mix ¾ cup plain seltzer water with ¼ cup pomegranate juice for a "homemade soda" that's much healthier than store-bought.
- Add pomegranate seeds to your regular or Greek yogurt, cold cereal, or oatmeal.
- Add pomegranate seeds to your favorite guacamole recipe.

Strawberries

Strawberries are a favorite fruit among many. Strawberry season varies depending on the part of the country you live in, with greater in-season availability in the south and on the west coast. In the northeast, strawberries are in season in June and July.

Nutrition highlights

One cup of whole strawberries contains just 46 calories and 11 grams of carbohydrate, including 3 grams of fiber. Strawberries provide more than 100 percent of your daily Vitamin C needs.

Healthy ideas

- Try one of my favorite summer salad recipes: baby spinach, sliced strawberries, pecans, grilled chicken, raspberry vinaigrette, and a sprinkling of chia seeds. This has tons of vitamins, minerals, fiber, and omega-3's, and is a great off-season meal when you're looking to cut down on calories.
- Any smoothie tastes great with strawberries. Blend different fruits with milk, yogurt, or unsweetened almond milk as a base. Then mix it up with ingredients like spinach/kale, ground flaxseeds, nuts, protein powder, peanut butter, or more.

- Instead of a peanut butter and banana sandwich, try a peanut butter and sliced strawberry sandwich.
- Add chopped strawberries to whole wheat quick bread and muffin recipes.
- Try making your own strawberry jam. An easy way to do this is by heating a pound of pureed strawberries on the stovetop with a few tablespoons of chia seeds and a tablespoon of sweetener. The chia seeds thicken the mixture for an easy and quick jam. Store in the refrigerator for several days.

Watermelon
Watermelon is the quintessential summertime fruit and a hydration superstar.

Nutrition highlights
One watermelon wedge contains 86 calories and 22 grams of carbohydrate. It's also got more than 30 percent of your daily Vitamin A and C needs, and about 10 percent of your daily potassium needs. Watermelon contains lycopene, a phytochemical and antioxidant. And, like it says in the name, it's got lots of water! In fact, 92 percent of the fruit is made of water, making it great for hydration.

Healthy ideas
- Combine mixed greens with shrimp, chopped watermelon, feta cheese and top with a balsamic vinaigrette. This unique salad sounds a bit odd, but the flavors meld together wonderfully.
- Layer yogurt, watermelon, blueberries, and breakfast cereal for a morning meal.
- Add watermelon to your favorite smoothie recipes.
- If you've had a grueling workout, watermelon sprinkled with salt might come as a refreshing hydrator and sodium/potassium-replenishing treat.

TL;DR Tips on Fruit:

- Fruits provide healthy carbohydrates along with tons of vitamins, minerals, phytochemicals, and antioxidants.
- If you struggle with eating fruit as a snack, the easiest way to increase your intake is by adding it to foods you already eat.
- Some suggestions include adding fruit to your smoothie, oatmeal, cold cereal, quick bread/muffin mixes, and salads.

Vegetables

Vegetables should make up a big portion of your plate at most meals. In fact, athletes should aim for a minimum of 2 ½ cups of vegetables each day – but some need considerably more! All vegetables are important for health, providing us with rich sources of vitamins, minerals, and phytochemicals. In this section of the book we'll be focusing on the vegetables that are richer in carbohydrates to help provide energy for your training. <u>However, keep in mind that other low calorie vegetables are of the utmost importance to a balanced diet, and you'll want to include these regularly!</u> This section in no way aims to shift the focus off of those choices. I simply want to share which vegetables are higher in carbohydrates, as that's the focus of this chapter.

Beets
Quick – what vegetable can really keep up the rhythm? Beets! (Haha.) Beets are a root vegetable, like carrots or potatoes, and come in several different varieties and colors. You can eat beets raw or cooked, and they are nutritious either way.

Nutrition highlights
One cup of cooked beet slices contains 74 calories and 17 grams of carbohydrate, including 4 grams of fiber. It's also got 34 percent of your daily folate needs and many phytonutrients, including a unique class of phytonutrients called betalains that act as antioxidants.

Healthy ideas:
- Add cooked beets to any smoothie. You probably won't even notice it's in there, and it helps boost the nutritional value.
- Roast fresh beets, drizzle with a tiny bit of olive oil, add salt and pepper, and enjoy.

- Add beets to your favorite stir fry recipe for a boost of color and phytonutrients.
- Cook couscous, and then toss with cooked beets and sautéed spinach.
- Add raw sliced beets to any salad.
- Slice beets thin and toss in olive oil, then bake to make "beet chips."

Carrots
Carrots are inexpensive and convenient for many athletes to use in meals and snacks.

Nutrition highlights
One cup of carrot strips contains 50 calories and 12 grams of carbohydrate, along with over 400 percent of your daily Vitamin A needs, 12 percent of your daily Vitamin C needs, and 390 mg of potassium.

Healthy ideas
- Shred carrots in your favorite whole wheat quick bread and muffin recipes.
- Add chopped/shredded carrots to stir fries with other veggies; serve over brown rice.
- Roast carrots in the oven with butternut squash and onions. Once tender, mix with vegetable broth in a large pot and use an immersion blender to puree into a creamy soup.
- Eat carrots and hummus for a healthy, filling snack.

Corn
Corn is another vegetable that can be a great addition to an athlete's plate. Plus, in the summer it's super inexpensive, making it a great cost-efficient way to eat what your body needs.

Nutrition highlights

A medium ear of corn contains 111 calories and 26 grams of carbohydrate. It also contains 3 grams of protein, a handful of B vitamins, and the antioxidants lutein and zeaxanathin, which contribute to eye health.

Healthy ideas

- Did you know that you can eat raw corn on the cob? This tastes best when it comes from a local farmer's market, so you know that it's super fresh. Just shuck it and eat it! It's got a delicious sweet taste that makes a great snack in the summer.
- Throw corn on the cob on the grill, and spice it up with your favorite seasonings like chili powder or cumin.
- Try this quick and hearty salad that's perfect for a single serving at lunch: mix ½ a pint of cherry tomatoes (or more if you like!), ½ a chopped avocado, a spoonful of chopped cilantro, ½ cup of black beans, and the corn you've removed from a small ear (or half a large ear). Sprinkle with cumin and enjoy!
- Try a creamy gnocchi: cook corn and garlic in a skillet for a few minutes, then add milk and a little parmesan cheese. Add cooked gnocchi and fresh arugula, and serve.

Potatoes

Regular potatoes have gotten a bad reputation over the past few years. On the contrary, potatoes can be a great addition to your meals as long as they are prepared in the proper way. You know as well as I do that French fries and potato chips are not going to be healthy choices when eaten frequently. But baked potatoes and boiled potatoes are actually great choices for athletes! The key is to cook potatoes without much additional fat, and also avoid adding additional fat later through toppings like butter or sour cream.

Nutrition highlights
One medium potato (flesh and skin) contains 160 calories, 37 grams of carbohydrate, and 4 grams of protein. You'll also get 4 grams of fiber, 28 percent of the daily value for vitamin C, and 10 percent of your daily iron needs. Not to mention a whopping 926 mg of potassium – about double the amount in a banana!

Quick tip
Did you know you can make a "baked" potato in the microwave? Poke a few holes with a fork, place it in a bowl, and cover with a wet paper towel. Cook it on high for six minutes, and then turn it over and cook it for another few minutes. When it's easy to cut, it's done.

Healthy ideas
- Top a baked potato with salsa instead of sour cream. You'll cut back on the fat of the sour cream and add extra vitamins and minerals from the tomatoes, onions, and peppers in the salsa.
- Make a healthy vegetarian or turkey chili, complete with lots of veggies and beans, and top a baked potato with a scoop of chili for dinner.
- Toss chopped potatoes, sweet potatoes, squash, and carrots with some olive oil and Italian seasoning or rosemary, and then roast in the oven.
- If you're a big fan of mashed potatoes, use fat free milk, light sour cream and/or reduced fat yogurt in your recipes, rather than calorie-laden cream. Add garlic and parsley for a tasty kick.
- Make a healthier version of home fries by mixing potatoes, peppers, and onions and sautéing in just a small amount of olive oil. Sometimes people complain that the potatoes don't cook quick enough this way, so my trick is microwaving the potato for a few minutes to pre-cook it,

and then chopping it up. This way, it doesn't need an overly long time in the skillet and you can use less oil.
- Add potatoes to your favorite soup recipes.

Pumpkin
It's not just for Halloween – in fact, pumpkin (whether you're cooking it fresh or buying it canned) is a great food to use year round.

Nutrition highlights
One cup of cooked, mashed fresh pumpkin contains 49 calories and 12 grams of carbohydrate, including 3 grams of dietary fiber to support digestive health. It also contains over 200 percent of your daily Vitamin A needs and 565 mg – or 16 percent - of your daily potassium needs.

Quick tip
Canned pumpkin is an excellent source of nutrients and is a wonderful alternative to roasting your own pumpkin (especially for quick recipes!). Look for canned versions that are pure pumpkin, not "pumpkin pie filling," which typically contains added sugar.

Healthy ideas
- Add pumpkin to whole wheat pancake, waffle, quick bread, or muffin mixes for a boost of nutrition.
- Love smoothies? Try an autumn-themed smoothie made with milk (or almond/soy milk), pumpkin, banana, cinnamon, and ice cubes. You can also add in some flax seeds or chia seeds for extra omega-3's.
- Dice fresh pumpkin and roast with sweet potatoes, potatoes, carrots, and/or butternut squash for a fall veggie feast.
- Add pumpkin puree to creamy pasta sauces (made with milk instead of cream, of course) for extra nutrition and flavor.

Sweet potatoes

There's much more to sweet potatoes than the Thanksgiving marshmallow casserole. These versatile veggies can be used in side dishes and main entrées alike.

Nutrition highlights

A medium sweet potato contains 100 calories and 24 grams of carbohydrate, including 4 grams of fiber. An eyesight superstar, this provides over 400 percent of your daily Vitamin A needs in the form of beta carotene. You'll also get 37 percent of your daily Vitamin C needs and 15 percent of your daily potassium needs.

Healthy ideas
- Use sweet potato in the same way you'd use a regular potato – baked, mashed, etc.
- Try making your own roasted sweet potatoes – cut them into strips or chunks and toss in olive oil and Italian seasoning. Roast in a 400 degree oven until tender. Time will vary based on the number of potatoes and the size of your cut.
- Top a baked sweet potato with black beans or ground turkey/beef, broccoli, and salsa – and ta-da! You've got a well-balanced meal that's easy and cheap.
- Add pureed cooked sweet potato to the batter for whole wheat pancakes, waffles, French toast, or quick breads.
- Instead of chicken enchiladas, try a sweet potato and black bean filling.

TL;DR Tips on Vegetables

- Vegetables rich in carbohydrates, as well as other nutrients, include choices like beets, carrots, corn, potatoes, pumpkin,

and sweet potatoes. Peas and winter squash also fit this
category.
- You should always include other lower calorie vegetables –
  like greens, tomatoes, asparagus, peppers, mushrooms, and
  more – in your meal plan each day, as these provide a
  variety of nutrients.
- Easy ways to eat more vegetables include using them in stir
  fries, roasting them as a side dish, mixing them into pasta,
  pureeing them into sauces and smoothies, or making a
  vegetarian entrée.

Beans

Red beans, kidney beans, black beans, pinto beans....the varieties are endless! Beans are a nutritional powerhouse and extremely inexpensive for all the benefits they provide. But most people don't eat them frequently – or at all. On average, Americans only eat about 1/3 cup of beans each week – far short of the 2010 Dietary Guidelines goal at least 1 ½ cups each week.

Nutrition highlights
The nutrition facts for beans will vary based on the type, but in general they are a super choice since they are...

1) *Full of fiber.* Beans contain about 6 to 8 grams of fiber per half cup.

2) *A good source of antioxidants.* Most people think of foods like fruit and tea as being rich in antioxidants, but beans pack a potent dose of antioxidants as well.

3) *Rich in nutrients.* A half cup of most beans provides an array of important nutrients, including iron (which works in your blood to carry oxygen throughout the body), magnesium, and folate.

4) *A good source of plant-based protein.* When we think of protein-rich foods, we often think of chicken, fish, and beef. But a half cup of beans provides 6 to 10 grams of protein.

5) *Rich in healthy carbohydrates.* A half cup of beans contains around 20-25 grams of energy-providing carbohydrate, depending on the type.

Quick tip
Dried beans are typically cheaper, but require more preparation work since you have to soak them in advance. Canned beans are a bit more expensive and contain additional sodium, but easy to use and a convenient pantry staple.

Beans, beans, they're good for your heart...
We all know the rest of this rhyme. There are two contributors to intestinal gas that some experience when consuming beans: 1) the overall increased fiber intake and 2) a type of carbohydrate called oligosaccharides.

To address the first issue, whenever you try to increase the amount of fiber in your diet, you also want to be sure you increase your fluid intake. Increasing fiber without increasing fluid can result in constipation and gas.

With regards to the second issue, your body processes oligosaccharides differently than other types of carbohydrate. In fact, the human body cannot actually break down these sugars – we lack the enzyme to do so. Instead, bacteria in your intestines actually break them down which produces gas. The good news is that your body can become more accustomed to this process, and it won't produce so much intestinal discomfort. If you find that you experience a lot of gas when eating beans, you can try one of the over-the-counter products designed to alleviate gas from beans. These contain an enzyme that breaks down oligosaccharides (note – if you have type 2 diabetes or mold allergies, these products may not be appropriate for you).

Healthy ideas
- Add beans to Mexican style dishes like burritos, tacos, or enchiladas. Avoid refried beans, though, which are made with lard.

- Top a salad with beans for a boost of filling fiber and protein.
- Make "beans & greens" – sauté collard greens, mustard greens, kale, or spinach with garlic, and add in your favorite type of beans.
- Puree black beans in a food processor with garlic, chopped onion, lemon juice, and cilantro to make a dip that you can use for baked tortilla chips or veggies.
- Add beans to just about any chili recipe and many soup recipes.
- Add pureed white beans to mashed potatoes.

TL;DR Tips on Beans

- Beans are a good source of carbohydrates, as well as fiber, protein, and micronutrients.
- Aim for 1 ½ cups or more of beans per week.
- If you eat beans often, your body can typically get used to them, resulting in less intestinal discomfort and gas.

Dairy

Dairy products are important to an athlete's diet, as they contain both carbohydrate and protein, along with calcium. However, if you are lactose intolerant or prefer to not use dairy products, there are certainly ways to meet your needs without eating from this category.

Milk

Skim or 1 percent milk is a great choice as part of an athlete's diet. Not only does a cup contain 12 grams of carbohydrate, but it also provides about 30 percent of your daily calcium needs and 8 grams of protein.

If you do not drink regular dairy milk, soy milk or almond milk are potential substitutes, though they have somewhat different nutrient profiles. For example, soymilk typically provides 6 grams of protein per serving, and almond milk usually has 0 to 1 grams compared to the 8 grams in dairy milk. Also, the type of calcium in milk substitutes may not be absorbed as well as the calcium in dairy milk. However, if you prefer or need to use milk substitutes, you can generally still meet your calcium and protein needs by making informed dietary choices throughout the day.

Yogurt

Yogurt is another great choice, and different types have different nutritional profiles. Some overarching nutritional highlights of yogurt include:

1) *Probiotic power* – Yogurt contains live cultures of "healthy bacteria." These cultures are thought to help with digestion, particularly in situations like after taking a round of antibiotics, which may have killed good bacteria along with the bad.

2) *Bone builder* – Yogurt is a great source of calcium. A 6 ounce serving of most regular yogurt provides 30-40 percent and a 6 ounce serving of most Greek yogurts provides 15-20 percent.

3) *Suitable for some people with mild lactose intolerance* - Even though yogurt contains lactose (the sugar found in milk) some people with mild forms of lactose intolerance can tolerate yogurt, particularly Greek style, without symptoms. The live cultures in the yogurt may help people digest it better.

4) *Great for muscles* – 6 ounces of regular yogurt typically contains around 8 grams of protein. And that same size serving of Greek yogurt can pack in 15-20 grams of protein. That's about the same amount in a 2-3 ounce serving of meat!

Selecting the right yogurt

- Avoid hype words or phrases. You may see these related to the probiotics – some yogurts will print "helps your digestive system!" or something similar – and then knock up the price for these claims. But almost all yogurt contains live cultures (that's the nature of how it's made). Simply look on the label for the fine print where it will say "contains live cultures." This means it has probiotic properties, even if it doesn't say anything about digestion on the package.

- Check labels for "fruit on the bottom" blends. These often have fruit in a concentrated sugary syrup – which means lots of added sugars. Instead, add your own fruit, or look for fruit-flavored varieties that don't have as much added sugar.

- Check the ingredients for artificial sweeteners. Some of the "light" yogurts are artificially sweetened with splenda or aspartame in order to reduce the sugar content and lower the calorie count. Consuming artificially sweetened food is a personal choice and your decision to do so may depend on your health goals.

- Yogurt varies in fat content based on the milk it was made with. Whole milk yogurts typically have a 3.25 percent fat content (about 8 grams per 8 ounce serving), low fat yogurts often have a 1 percent fat content (about 2 to 3 grams of fat per 8 ounce serving), and non-fat yogurts are made from skim milk with no fat. Choose low fat or non-fat yogurts to cut down on calories and saturated fat.

TL;DR Tips on Dairy

- Milk and yogurt (both regular and Greek) provide carbohydrate along with protein and calcium.
- Regular yogurt contains more calcium but less protein compared to Greek yogurt.
- If you don't like dairy or can't eat it, you can still meet all your nutrient needs with other carefully planned choices.

Power Up
With Protein

Power up with Protein

Protein is also essential to any athlete's diet. It's one of the three macronutrients that provide calories, and it has several functions in the body:

- Helps with muscle building and recovery
- Supports development of hair, skin, and nails
- Provides enzymes that regulate body functions
- Helps with transportation of nutrients and oxygen throughout body

How much do I need?

Getting enough protein is a careful balance. Eating too much of any macronutrient – including protein – can contribute to excess calories and weight gain. Or, if you're focusing too much on protein intake, you may not be getting enough carbohydrate or essential fats. And if you eat too many animal protein foods, you may also get excessive amounts of saturated fat, which could contribute to heart problems. However, consuming too little protein will result in compromised training and muscular recovery.

Many Americans get more protein than they actually need each day, but some athletes don't meet their needs. About 10-20 percent of your calories each day should come from protein, with specific amounts based on your weight and training level. To figure out how much protein you need each day, consider the estimates in the chart on the following page.

Protein Recommendations Based on Training Volume:

Training Volume	Protein Recommendations
Most adults; including those who are sedentary and those who exercise lightly for fitness/health	0.8 grams protein per kilogram to 1 gram per kilogram
Light to moderate endurance training	1.2 to 1.7 grams protein per kilogram
Heavy endurance training and high intensity (4-5+ hours of training per day)	1.4 to 2 grams protein per kilogram

*Developed using AND (2013); ADA & ACSM (2009); IOC (2004)

In order to calculate your needs, you can take your weight in pounds and divide it by 2.2 to find out your weight in kilograms. Then, multiply by the factor above that is closest to your lifestyle.

Example: 150 pound female, exercises at a light to moderate intensity 3 times a week for health
- 150 pounds / 2.2 = 68.2 kilograms
- 68.2 x 0.8 = 55 grams of protein
- 68.2 x 1 = 68 grams of protein
- 55 to 68 grams of protein per day would be a good amount for this individual

Example: 200 pound male, trains for endurance sports one to three hours per day
- 200 pounds / 2.2 = 90.9 kilograms
- 90.9 kg x 1.2 = 109 grams of protein
- 90.9 x 1.7 = 155 grams of protein
- 109 to 155 grams of protein would be a good amount for this individual

From here, you can select an amount from the higher or lower end of the range that you feel is most appropriate for your level of training.

If you're an athlete that's trying to lose weight, you may want to choose a number towards the middle to high end of the appropriate range. When your body is in a caloric deficit, you can start to break down a small amount of lean mass during moderate and high training loads. We want to avoid this as much as possible, and eating enough protein can help to maintain muscle mass during training.

What types of protein foods should I eat?

Meats, fish, poultry, eggs, dairy products, beans, seeds and nuts are all good sources of protein. Whole grains also contain some protein.

While animal sources are complete proteins (meaning they contain all the essential amino acids you need), plant sources of protein can meet your needs too. Vegetarians should simply make sure they eat a variety of different sources of plant proteins for optimal health. By eating a variety of beans, nuts, seeds, legumes, and whole grains, vegetarian athletes can meet their protein needs.

The chart on the following page shows the amount of protein in common foods.

I always recommend whole foods like those mentioned above for meeting your protein needs when possible. However, occasionally I'll have a client who has trouble meeting their protein needs and the traditional sources don't appeal to them. In this case, there are protein powders that can be used to boost your intake (for example, in an afternoon smoothie snack). These come in varieties made from milk (whey protein) and egg, as well as vegan protein powders which are typically made from soy, peas, or hemp.

Protein in Common Foods:

Food	Protein in grams
3 ounces of cooked chicken breast	27
3 ounces of cooked hamburger meat or lean beef	25
3 ounces of cooked pork loin	23
3 ounces of cooked fish	22
1 scoop of commercial protein powders (whey, soy, etc.)	20 to 25
6 ounces of Greek yogurt	15 to 20
½ cup of cottage cheese	12 to 14
½ cup tofu	10
1 cup of regular yogurt	8 to 10
1 cup of cooked quinoa	8
¼ cup of almonds	8
1 cup of skim milk	8
1 ounce of cheddar cheese	7
½ cup of beans	6 to 10
1 large egg	6
1 cup of brown rice	5
2 slices of whole wheat bread	4

*Developed using the USDA Nutrient Database

You can see that it's pretty easy for most people to meet their needs by simply eating a variety of foods. In addition, take note that the portion sizes for meats are relatively small. Three ounces of meat is only about the size of a deck of cards – far less than many people serve themselves at one time – meaning you may get much more protein than you realize if you are consuming larger portions.

Consider a day with these meals:

Meal/Snack	Foods	Protein
Breakfast	1 cup of cereal 1 cup of skim milk Banana	3 grams 8 grams
Snack	Apple 2 tbsp peanut butter	8 grams
Lunch	Salad: Leafy greens 4 ounces grilled chicken ¼ cup almonds 1 cup strawberries Sweet potato on the side	36 grams 8 grams 2 grams
Dinner	Stir fry: 1 cup cooked brown rice 4 ounces lean beef 2 cups mixed vegetables	4 grams 29 grams
Total		98 grams

That's more than enough for most adults, including many athletes. For example, a 68 kilogram (150 pound) person would be eating about 1.4 g/kg of protein with the meals above – definitely in our range for endurance athletes doing light to moderate training.

Most athletes can easily meet their protein needs each day without a lot of extra work, as they're eating large quantities of food. If you tend to fall short in your protein needs, add some small amounts of protein rich items to your meals or snacks.

TL;DR Tips on Protein

- Protein is important for muscular growth and recovery.

- Daily protein needs are based on your weight and training volume, and should generally make up about 10-20 percent of daily calories.
- Meats, fish, poultry, eggs, dairy products, beans, seeds and nuts are all good sources of protein.

The Skinny on Fats

The skinny on fats

In the 1980s and 1990s, fat became a scary word for many people. Large organizations were promoting low fat diets in the name of heart health, and aisles of "fat free cookies" and "low fat cake" grew rampant in the supermarket (ugh – bad memories!). Of course, we now know that not all fats are equal. Many types of fat are actually good for us. Fat helps us to absorb vitamins, promotes satiety after eating, and certain types actually promote heart health.

The Good

In this category are unsaturated fats, including monounsaturated and polyunsaturated fats. Monounsaturated fats are found in foods like olive and canola oil, nuts, avocados, and pumpkin seeds. Polyunsaturated fats are found in foods like soybean and corn oils, walnuts, fish, and flax seeds. One type of polyunsaturated fat called omega-3 fatty acids, found mainly in fish and flax/chia seeds, is thought to be particularly good for heart and brain health.

Research shows that when people replace either saturated fat or some refined carbohydrates with mono or polyunsaturated fats, it helps decrease LDL ("bad") cholesterol (Siri-Tarino et al, 2010). When there is too much LDL cholesterol in the blood, it can stick to the walls of the arteries. This narrows the arteries, reduces blood flow, and can eventually result in heart attack or stroke. Thus, lowering LDL cholesterol through the right fat choices can improve heart health.

Let's look more in detail at two types of oils high in unsaturated fats that are useful for cooking:
- *Olive oil* has the highest amount of heart healthy mono-unsaturated fats among common oils, but doesn't have many omega-3 fatty acids. It's versatile for cooking and great for dressings. You can substitute olive oil in certain baked goods, but some people find it may give the food a

slight olive flavor. Olive oil can't be heated to too hot a temperature for activities like frying (which I hope you're not doing too much of anyway), or it'll start to smoke.

- *Canola oil* is probably one of the most versatile oils, as it can be used for high temperature cooking as well as baking. It's got the least amount of saturated fat, high levels of monounsaturated fat (though not as high as olive oil), and more omega-3 fatty acids compared to other vegetable oils. Some people use caution with canola oil since it is one of the most commonly genetically modified (GMO) products on the market. Though the research on GMO products is still scarce, some researchers believe these products may contribute to certain health problems. If you are concerned about this, you can search for a non-GMO canola oil.

The Bad

Saturated fats are found mainly in animal products like red meats, chicken/turkey with skin, and dairy products. They're also found in coconut oil and palm oil. Saturated fats raise HDL ("good") cholesterol but also raise LDL ("bad") cholesterol, so it's better to get our fats from unsaturated sources. That being said, certain types of saturated fat may be better for us than others.

Coconut oil has gotten a lot of play in the media lately for being a "healthier alternative" to traditional oils, or being a "weight loss oil." While coconut oil is by no means a "miracle food," it's also not quite as unhealthy as we once thought. It does actually contain very high levels of saturated fat – 92 percent (which is higher than butter)! But new research shows the specific type of saturated fat in coconut oil may not affect cholesterol the same way as the other types of saturated fat (Feranil et al, 2011; Assuncao et al, 2009). Of course, it's high in calories just like any other oil, though, and should be used in moderation.

The Ugly

Trans fats are created when liquid oils undergo a process called partial hydrogenation. This process makes the fat more shelf-stable, less likely to spoil, and able to withstand repeated heating and frying without breaking down. However, the fat created is especially bad for us since it raises LDL ("bad") cholesterol *and* lowers HDL ("good") cholesterol. According to Harvard Medical School, for every 2 percent of calories that you eat daily from trans fat, your risk of heart disease goes up by 23 percent. That's a pretty staggering statistic and a good reason for any athlete to steer clear of them. Heart problems would most definitely put a damper on any training season.

How much fat should I eat?

Fats, mostly of the healthy mono and polyunsaturated type, should make up about 20-30 percent of the calories in your diet. We need them to help absorb vitamins and to feel full! And while saturated fats can contribute to some cardiovascular risk factors, newer research shows that when people replace these with refined carbohydrates, there is actually a greater risk of cardiovascular disease (Siri-Tarino et al, 2010). Replacing saturated fats with unsaturated fats is a better strategy. As for trans fats, keep your intake as low as possible, since these pose the greatest risk to your health.

With any type of fat, though, keep in mind that it is a more calorie dense option – providing 9 calories per gram, compared to the 4 calories per gram found in protein and carbohydrate. If you eat too much fat each day, you may also be pushing out the healthy carbohydrates you need to fuel your training or the protein you need for muscular strength and recovery. Keep a proper balance with the right types of fat for optimal health!

TL'DR Tips on Fat

- Mono and polyunsaturated fats are healthy. These are found in foods like olive oil, fish, nuts, and avocadoes.
- Saturated fats are not great for your body, and trans fats are the worst for your body.
- About 20-30 percent of your calories should come from healthy sources of fat.

Micronutrients
for Optimal Health

Micronutrients for Optimal Health

Vitamins & Minerals

In addition to our three macronutrients – carbohydrate, protein, and fat – this book would not be complete without talking about micronutrients. Micronutrients refer to vitamins and minerals, that although are needed in smaller amounts (hence micro vs. macro), are still extremely important to overall health and athletic performance. The following are the essential micronutrients our body needs:

Vitamins:	Minerals:
Vitamin A	**Calcium**
Vitamin C	Chloride
Vitamin D	Chromium
Vitamin E	Copper
Vitamin K	Flouride
B Vitamins – Thiamin, Riboflavin, Niacin, Pantothenic Acid, Vitamin B6, Folate, Vitamin B12, Biotin	Iodine
	Iron
	Magnesium
	Manganese
	Molybdenum
	Phosphorus
	Potassium
	Selenium
	Sodium
	Sulfur
	Zinc

While each one of these is no doubt important, for the purposes of this book we are going to focus on the bolded micronutrients. Each of these either commonly comes up short in many peoples' diets, or is particularly important to athletes.

Should I supplement?

An athlete eating a proper diet should be able to meet all their micronutrient needs through food. Getting nutrients through food is most beneficial, as the nutrients may work synergistically with other vitamins, minerals, and phytochemicals in the food. In addition, while it is unlikely to reach toxic levels of vitamins and minerals in the body through food consumption, it is possible to experience toxicity with excessive supplementation.

If you are struggling to meet your needs, there is typically no harm in taking a standard multivitamin. Depending on your medical needs, other supplements may be appropriate – for example, calcium or Vitamin D – but **check with your doctor** before beginning any supplement. Avoid mega-doses of vitamins and minerals, as these may cause harm (McGinley et al, 2009).

Vitamin C

Vitamin C has long been promoted as an immune booster. For example, have you ever been told to gulp down some orange juice when you're sick? Though the research on Vitamin C and prevention of the common cold isn't quite as strong as we'd once hoped, we do know that Vitamin C is essential for a healthy immune system and no doubt important for athletes in training. It's important to get lots of Vitamin-C rich foods in your diet each day, since your body cannot make Vitamin C or store extra amounts of Vitamin C.

Functions

Vitamin C has many roles in the body, including:
- Healing wounds and helping prevent major bruising
- Forming scar tissue
- Forming a protein that's important to the structure of skin, ligaments and cartilage
- Act as an antioxidant in the body, possibly contributing to reduced disease risk

94

- Helping your body to better absorb plant-based sources of iron

Does Vitamin C prevent colds?
The latest research shows that getting Vitamin C at or over the recommended daily amount likely doesn't prevent the number of colds that the general population gets each year. However, it seems that among endurance athletes, Vitamin C *may* play a role in reducing the number of colds each year (Douglas et al, 2007). In addition, it may shorten the duration of the cold or reduce the intensity of the symptoms.

How much do I need?
The recommended daily intake for Vitamin C is 90 mg/day for men and 75 mg/day for women.

Where do I get it?
The best sources are fruits and vegetables, and the following are some great choices from both categories:

Vegetables	Vitamin C	Fruits	Vitamin C
Red peppers, sliced (1 cup)	118 mg	Small papaya	96 mg
Brussels sprouts (1 cup)	97 mg	Strawberries (1 cup)	85 mg
Raw broccoli, chopped (1 cup)	81 mg	Naval orange	83 mg
Green peppers, sliced (1 cup)	74 mg	Pineapple, chopped (1 cup)	79 mg
Kale, cooked (1 cup)	27 mg	Kiwi	64 mg

*Developed using USDA Nutrient Database

Vitamin D

Vitamin D has long been known for its role in the quest to build strong bones. Your body requires Vitamin D to help absorb calcium; they work as a team. When your blood levels of calcium start to fall short, your body converts Vitamin D to its active form, where it travels to the intestines to increase calcium absorption and to the kidneys to "tell them" to conserve calcium losses in the urine. Researchers suggest that adequate Vitamin D may be particularly important for athletes, alluding to a potentially decreased risk of stress fractures and muscle injuries (Angeline et al, 2013; Hamilton, 2011).

How much do I need?

The recommendation for adults age 19-70 is 600 IU of Vitamin D per day. Some professionals feel that certain individuals may need more than this amount, but there is no definitive consensus. If you're concerned about your Vitamin D levels, you can have them checked at a doctor's office.

Where do I get it?

Vitamin D is a bit more difficult to get in our diet (compared to other nutrients) since it's only found naturally in a few foods. These include fatty fish, egg yolks, cheese, and liver. There is also Vitamin D in fortified foods like cereals, milk, and some orange juices, which can be used to increase your intake.

Your body makes Vitamin D from sunlight too through a reaction in your skin. However, this only occurs in skin that has not been treated with sunscreen. Even an SPF of 8, sometimes added to moisturizers or lotions, can reduce Vitamin D production by 95 percent according to the National Osteoporosis Foundation. Skipping sunscreen and exposing your skin to UVB rays is risky, though, since it increases the risk of skin cancer.

You can certainly meet your vitamin D needs if you are eating a variety of foods including those that are fortified. However, if you find it is difficult to get Vitamin D via your diet, and because sun exposure contributes to skin cancer risk, you may consider taking a Vitamin D supplement if you feel that you are not meeting your needs. Be sure to speak with your doctor before starting any new supplement.

Calcium

Calcium is essential for strong bones and reduced risk of osteoporosis. Almost all your calcium is stored in your bones and teeth – 99 percent to be exact. The rest of the calcium circulates throughout your blood and soft tissue. When you don't get enough calcium in your diet, your body has to pull it from your bones to ensure the calcium levels in your blood are tightly regulated. Over time, this can make your bones weak.

How much do I need?
The Institute of Medicine recommends:
- Males 19-70 – 1000 mg
- Females 19-50 – 1000 mg
- Females 50-70 – 1200 mg

Where do I get it?
Milk, yogurt, and cheese are great sources of calcium. But you can also get calcium from other natural sources, including dark green vegetables, like spinach, kale and collard greens, canned sardines (with the bones); or tofu. There are also foods that are fortified with calcium, like orange juice or cereals.

Iron

Iron deficiency is actually the most common nutrient deficiency around the world. While it is not as common in the US as other countries, there are people who may still fall short in their iron intake. Iron deficiency is more common among women, since they lose iron during their menstrual cycle each month.

Iron is of particular concern to you as a runner or triathlete, since iron deficiency can result in fatigue and poor performance. In your body, iron is used as a part of hemoglobin, which transports oxygen around your bloodstream to your cells. The reason many people with iron deficiency end up tired is because they are not able to get as much oxygen to all their cells.

How much do I need?
Recommendations vary based on age and gender:
- Men age 19-70+ - 8 mg/day
- Women age 19-50 – 18 mg/day
- Women age 51+ - 8 mg/day

Where do I get it?
There are two types of iron: heme and nonheme iron. Heme iron is found in animal products and is highly absorbable. Nonheme iron is found in plant products. It is not absorbed as well as heme iron. However, if you are a vegetarian, there are certain things you can do to increase the absorption of nonheme iron. For example, eating these plant sources of iron with a food rich in Vitamin C actually helps your body to absorb more. Along the same lines, if you are concerned about your iron status, you should avoid eating plant sources of iron with coffee, tea, or foods rich in calcium. The calcium and the tannins (found in the coffee or tea) actually interfere with iron absorption.

Following is a chart with examples of iron-rich foods that you can include in your diet.

Iron Rich Food Choices:

Animal sources:	Plant sources:
Chicken	Legumes (beans and lentils)
Turkey	Broccoli
Beef	Asparagus
Lamb	Brussels Sprouts
Pork	Potatoes
Many types of fish, like tuna, clams, shrimp, and salmon	Dried fruits, like raisins and apricots
Egg (found in the yolk)	Soybeans
	Nuts & seeds
	Iron-fortified whole grains (note that these contain phytates which reduces the amount of iron absorbed)
	Spinach and other greens (note that these contain oxalic acid which reduces the amount of iron absorbed)

Magnesium

Magnesium is a mineral found in many different food choices. While clinical magnesium deficiency is relatively rare in the United States, scientists have recently pointed to many potential protective roles of magnesium in the body. These include:

- *Blood pressure regulation* – Diets high in potassium, magnesium and fiber are associated with lower blood pressure. Diets of this nature are typically high in fruits, vegetables, low fat dairy, and nuts.
- *Bone health* – Magnesium may help maintain bone strength (Matias et al, 2012).
- *Migraine prevention/treatment* – New research and anecdotal evidence suggests that inadequate magnesium intake may

play a role in migraines (Tarighat et al, 2012). If you experience migraines, try monitoring your intake and see if increasing magnesium-rich foods helps.

How much do I need?
The recommended daily allowance for magnesium is as follows:
- Males 19-30 - 400 mg
- Males 31+ - 420 mg
- Females 19-30 – 310 mg
- Females 31+ - 320 mg

Where do I get it?
Leafy green vegetables, beans and legumes, low fat dairy, whole grains, and nuts/seeds are good sources of magnesium.

Here are some specific examples of the magnesium content of common foods:

Food	Magnesium
Prepared edamame, from frozen, 1 cup	99 mg
Almonds, 1 ounce	80 mg
Spinach, cooked, ½ cup	78 mg
Swiss chard, cooked, ½ cup	75 mg
Pumpkin seeds, 1 ounce (about 85 seeds)	74 mg
Bran flakes cereal, ¾ cup	64 mg
Oatmeal, 1 cup	61 mg
Peanut butter, 2 tbsp	49 mg
Baked potato with skin	49 mg
Black eyed peas, ½ cup	46 mg
Kidney beans, ½ cup	35 mg
Low fat milk, 1 cup	27 mg

*Developed using USDA Nutrient Database

Potassium

Potassium is an essential mineral that our bodies need. It's especially important for heart and muscle contractions, as well as proper functioning of the kidneys and digestive system.. Athletes have traditionally eaten potassium rich foods due to the theory that it may reduce muscle cramps. While there's not much definitive research that suggests this is true, anecdotal evidence often suggests otherwise. Plus, there are lots of other benefits to eating foods rich in potassium, including reduced risk of high blood pressure.

How much do I need?

The Institute of Medicine recommends that adults get at least 4,700 mg of potassium each day. It's important to note that most of the health benefits associated with the consumption of potassium are related to food, not supplements. There is no reason for most people to take a potassium supplement unless your doctor asks you to take one for a medical reason – and it could actually be dangerous, as excessively high potassium levels in the blood can cause irregular heart rhythms and possibly death. Stick to getting your potassium through what you eat!

Where do I get it?

Many foods contain potassium, including fruits, vegetables, meats, and dairy products. By eating a variety of foods each day you should be able to meet your needs. The chart on the next page shows great choices for potassium-rich foods that also provide additional important nutrients.

Sources of Potassium:

Food	Potassium Content	Additional Benefit
Pumpkin seeds, ¼ cup	261 mg	Great source of iron
Black beans, ½ cup	305 mg	Lots of fiber and some protein
Avocado, ½ of a whole one	345 mg	Good source of monounsaturated (heart healthy) fats
Prunes, 5 pitted	348 mg	Fiber to help your digestive system
Skim milk, 1 cup	382 mg	Calcium, Vitamin D, and protein
Salmon, 3 ounces	416 mg	Omega-3 fatty acids
Kiwi, 2 whole	430 mg	Lots of Vitamin C
Banana, large	485 mg	Healthy carbohydrates
Low fat yogurt, plain, 8 ounce container	531 mg	Calcium for strong bones
Sweet potato, medium	542 mg	Vitamin A for healthy eyesight
Beet greens, cooked, ½ cup	654 mg	Vitamin A for healthy eyesight
Apricots, dried, ½ cup	755 mg	Vitamin A for healthy eyesight
Potato, russet, small	759 mg	Good source of Vitamin C

*Developed using the USDA Nutrient Database

Zinc

Zinc has many functions, including involvement in maintaining proper eyesight, taste sensation, and our immune response. A review study that came out in 2011 concluded that zinc can help reduce the severity and duration of the common cold (Singh et al, 2011). Also, when people consumed zinc supplements over the long term, there was the potential to reduce the number of colds they got. However, supplements are not appropriate for everyone. A better strategy (as with most of our nutrients) is to stock up on zinc rich food choices.

How much do I need?
The Institute of Medicine recommends 11 mg per day for men and 8 mg per day for women.

Where can I get it?
Good sources of zinc include nuts, seeds, meat, shellfish, oats, yogurt, and fortified cereal.

TL;DR Tips on Vitamins and Minerals

- It is generally better to get micronutrients through foods rather than supplements.
- Depending on your diet and medical history, a multivitamin, calcium, Vitamin D, and/or iron (particularly for women) supplement may be appropriate. Speak with a doctor or dietitian before beginning any supplement, as getting too much of any nutrient can be dangerous.
- The following vitamins and minerals are important to athletes or often come up short in diets, and here's where you can find them in foods:
  - Vitamin C – fruits and vegetables

- Vitamin D – fatty fish, egg yolks, liver, fortified dairy products, fortified cereals
- Calcium – dairy products, leafy green vegetables, tofu, fortified foods
- Iron – meats, fish, legumes, some vegetables, dried fruits
- Magnesium – leafy green vegetables, beans and legumes, low fat dairy, whole grains, and nuts/seeds
- Potassium – fruits and vegetables, meat, dairy
- Zinc - nuts, seeds, meat, shellfish, oats, yogurt, and fortified cereals

Phytochemicals

Though not considered essential micronutrients, phytochemicals should be an important part of an athlete's diet. Phytochemicals are plant components other than vitamins and minerals which may also promote optimal health. Scientists have discovered thousands of phytochemicals but are just beginning to understand how some of them work. In addition, it appears that some phytochemicals may work in synergy with each other when eaten regularly.

Each color fruit and vegetable contains unique phytochemicals. Here are some examples:

Red fruits and vegetables contain several different types of phytochemicals. Lycopene may help reduce the risk of certain types of cancer (Yang et al, 2013; Sharoni et al, 2012). It is found in tomatoes, grapefruit, and watermelon. Anthocyanins act as antioxidants in the body, and are found in foods like berries and grapes. Proanthocyanidins are found in high concentration in cranberries, which may contribute to urinary tract health (Rossi et al, 2010).

Yellow/orange fruits and vegetables contain carotenoids. In particular, many are high in beta-carotene, which is used to form Vitamin A in the body to support eyesight. Sweet potatoes, carrots, squash, mangoes, and pumpkin are good sources of beta carotene. Citrus fruits like lemons and oranges also contain flavanones, which may reduce cardiovascular disease risk (Chanet et al, 2012).

Green fruits and vegetables may contain lutein. The American Optometric Association supports eating foods rich in lutein to supports proper eyesight. Leafy greens, peppers, cucumbers, and celery contain lutein. Vegetables like broccoli, Brussels sprouts, and cabbage contain isothiocyanates, which may help prevent cancer (ACS, 2008).

Blue and purple fruits and vegetables contain anthocyanins, similar to certain red produce. Anthocyanins are found in blueberries, blackberries, and grapes. These powerful antioxidants may reduce the risk of heart disease and cancer. Certain anthocyanins like those in blueberries may also improve memory during aging (Shukitt-Hale, 2012).

White fruits and vegetables are important too! Garlic and onions contain allicin, which may help lower cholesterol and blood pressure (Reinhart et al, 2008; Ashraf et al, 2005).

What can I do to increase my phytochemical consumption?
Focus on the old mantra of "eat a rainbow!" By consuming a variety of colors and types of fruits and vegetables, you'll be consuming many different phytochemicals. Struggling with ways to create colorful meals or snacks full of fruits and veggies? Consider these five ideas, which each use a variety of colorful produce:

1) Develop a smoothie with items from several of the color categories. For example, combine strawberries, mango, blueberries, and spinach together with juice or milk.

2) Create a colorful salad. Start with spinach or mixed leafy greens, and then build your salad with more veggies - like carrots, tomatoes, cucumbers, bell peppers – and/or fruits – like strawberries, mandarin oranges, craisins, and grapes.

3) Build a burrito. Mix brown rice with black beans, corn, chopped bell peppers, onions, and tomatoes, and then add to a whole wheat wrap!

4) Roast garlic, eggplant, zucchini, bell peppers, and onions on a baking sheet. For a pasta dish, toss with chopped tomatoes, whole wheat pasta, olive oil, and parmesan

cheese. Or as an alternative, combine with mozzarella cheese in a whole wheat wrap.

5) Whip up a hearty chili with pinto beans, onions, garlic, zucchini, bell peppers, and tomatoes.

TL;DR Tips on Phytochemicals

- Phytochemicals are plant compounds that are good for your body.
- Eat produce in a variety of colors for a mixture of lots of phytochemicals, leading to optimal health and performance.

Hydration & Electrolytes

Hydration & Electrolytes

Keeping your body hydrated is important for all of us, as most of your body's insides are comprised of water. In fact, 45 to 75 percent of your body mass is made up of water. This amount varies mainly due to differences in body composition, since muscle mass contains a much higher proportion of water compared to fat mass (ACSM, 2007).

Water has many functions in the body: it moistens tissues (like those of the eyes and mouth), lubricates joints, maintains the correct body temperature, prevents constipation, and more. And hydration is especially important for athletes, since taking in too little or too much fluid can be dangerous and detrimental to performance. But how much water do we need to drink each day to keep our body functioning optimally? Should we drink only when we're thirsty? Follow the 8 glasses a day rule? Do some fancy calculations to figure out an individualized fluid intake? Let's find out.

How much water do I need each day?

Each day you lose water through breathing, sweating, and using the bathroom. In order to replace these losses, you must get fluid through foods and liquids. We'll get into exercise hydration guidelines in a minute, but let's start with our everyday daily hydration guidelines.

The following are the most current daily fluid recommendations from the Institute of Medicine/Dietary Reference Intakes (2010).
- Men: 16 cups (3.7 liters) of total water, with about 13 cups (3 liters) coming from beverage intake
- Women: 11.5 cups (2.7 liters) of total water, with about 9 cups (2.2 liters) coming from beverage intake

You can see that the "total water intake" differs from that which they recommend for "beverage intake," because we get about 20 percent of our water through foods we eat, like fruits and vegetables. This fluid from food contributes to the total water intake and is the reason for the discrepancy between the two numbers.

There's no need to worry about measuring out your daily water intake every day, though. If you drink by thirst, you should be fine. However, many people often ignore signs of thirst or mistake thirst for hunger. In this case, it may be worthwhile to measure your water consumption for a day or two and see if it's in line with the guidelines.

You can also get a good idea of your hydration status through the "pee test." The hard and fast rule: if your urine looks like apple juice, you probably need to hydrate more. If your urine looks like a diluted glass of lemonade, you're probably at the right hydration level.

Factors to consider
Certain factors can influence your hydration needs outside of these guidelines. These include:

- Weather – If you're outside in hot weather, you'll have increased water losses and will likely need additional fluid. Be sure to carry a water bottle with you on hot days.

- Illness – If you're vomiting or you have diarrhea, you're losing extra fluid. You also need extra fluids when you have a fever.

- Pregnancy or breastfeeding – Both of these require additional fluid intake each day.

- And of course, exercise - For intense exercise sessions lasting longer than an hour, you'll need more fluid and you'll also need to replace electrolytes. More on this in a second.

What counts towards my regular daily fluid needs?
While we know that water or sports drink is appropriate for exercise, during the remainder of the day other beverages can contribute to your daily needs. Milk, juices, coffee, tea, and sodas can be counted towards your fluid needs. Caffeinated versions, in moderation, do count (their diuretic effect is transient and doesn't impact the body's water balance majorly when consumed in small amounts). However, it is obvious that some of these choices – namely soda – are not a good everyday choice for maintaining health. Try to stick to water for the majority of your daily fluid intake. If you find it hard to drink plain water, consider these options:

- Add fruits or vegetables to a pitcher of water to give it some extra flavor. Try cucumbers, blueberries, lemons, or limes.
- Miss the bubbly soda? Try seltzer water. Look for flavored options that have no added sweeteners (regular or artificial), or buy plain seltzer and add the items in the last tip.
- If you drink a ton of fruit juice, consider diluting it in a ratio of ½ juice, ½ water. You'll save calories and still have a strong fruit taste. Or consider mixing it with seltzer for a faux "soda." Many people like some of the stronger juices, like pomegranate or grapefruit juice, mixed with seltzer in this way. I'll often mix ¼ cup grapefruit juice with another 1 cup of seltzer for a delicious option that almost tastes like soda.
- Carry a water bottle with you everywhere. You'll be surprised how much more you drink when you have it at your fingertips.

Hydration for Exercise

It is extremely important to pay attention to hydration during long training workouts and races. Too much fluid can lead to hyponatremia. Hyponatremia occurs when the sodium levels in blood drop too low leading to a bunch of not-so-fun consequences like nausea, vomiting, and disorientation in mild forms. In severe cases, there can be life-threatening complications including a buildup of excessive fluid in the brain and lungs, respiratory arrest, coma, and death.

Fluid overload is the primary factor leading to hyponatremia, especially in events lasting less than four hours. In events over four hours, fluid overload is still a primary cause but a lack of sodium intake can also play a role (Montain et al, 2006). During normal everyday hydration, your body can typically adjust for excessive hydration by increasing urine production. During exercise, however, this physiological mechanism is less effective and you aren't able to get rid of excess fluid as quickly (ACSM, 2007).

Along the same lines, too little fluid can result in dehydration. Dehydration is more common among athletes than hyponatremia. For example, among Boston Marathon runners from 2001-2008, those ending up in the medical tent were almost six times more likely to have dehydration compared to hyponatremia (Siegel et al, 2009).
Moderate dehydration can impair aerobic performance by increasing body temperature and heart rate, as well as increasing perceived exertion – aka making the exercise feel more difficult. Because heart rate increases, the body also relies on a greater percentage of carbohydrate as fuel, increasing the risk of running low on such fuel and "hitting the wall" earlier (Barr, 1999).

Let's look at an example of how dehydration might affect you. Pretend you practice your fueling plan during long runs or rides and you have developed a good balance between hydration, fuel, and the level of activity. But the day of your half Ironman comes and you didn't pay much attention to hydration that morning. Plus, you feel so great at the beginning of the race that you aren't really paying attention to your thirst, so you don't start drinking your sports drink until two hours into to event. Later in the race, you start feeling unbelievably fatigued even though from hour two until now you have been following the rate of hydration/carbohydrate intake you practiced. Because you didn't hydrate at the beginning, your body could be dehydrated. This can lead to an increased heart rate and cause you to rely on a higher proportion of carbohydrate for fuel (compared to your typical carbohydrate/fat utilization ratio).

What happens? Bam – you hit that wall earlier.

The greater the rate of dehydration the more severe the side effects will be. The specific percent dehydration that initiates a significant drop in aerobic performance varies between individuals based on an athlete's biological and physiological characteristics, the environmental temperature, and the type of specific exercise. However, researchers believe the decline in performance occurs for the majority of athletes when they lose enough fluid to cause a 2-3 percent loss of body weight. Some athletes may experience a decline in performance at a slightly lower percentage and others may be slightly more tolerant to the effects of dehydration (ACSM, 2007). The risk of poorer performance with dehydration is more likely in warm/hot weather conditions.

How much should I drink during exercise?
Knowing these facts, my advice is to maintain your hydration levels within approximately 2 percent of your normal body weight. For example, let's say you are a 170 pound athlete. A 2 percent loss in body weight would be the equivalent of losing about 3.5 pounds. During exercise, we would want you to avoid losing much more than 3.5 pounds (risk of dehydration impairing performance) as

well as avoid gaining any weight (risk of hyponatremia). It is not necessary to match your sweat loss rates exactly, as within that 2 percent guideline is adequate and helps avoid the risk of hyponatremia (IOC, 2004).

Right now, you might be wondering how you would know the amount you need to drink to prevent losing more than 2 percent. The short answer is using a hydration plan based on thirst and sweat test results. I'll explain more...

You see, it's a bit difficult to give precise hydration guidelines across the board, because the rate at which athletes sweat varies from one person to another and depends on multiple factors discussed earlier. The average athlete will lose between 0.5 liters to 2 liters of sweat per hour of exercise (ACSM, 2007). Body weight, genetics, and metabolic factors all affect your sweat rate (and the composition of that sweat). Along the same lines, warmer weather and heavier clothing items generally elicit a higher sweat rate when compared to exercising in cooler weather or lighter clothing (one of the reasons it's important to train in the right gear).

Up until a few years ago, there were various recommendations encouraging athletes to "stay ahead of your thirst." These concepts are "old-school" hydration, and have been debunked most famously by researcher and author Timothy Noakes. He makes reference to the fact that when the methodology of "staying ahead of your thirst" and "drinking as much as you can" become popular, cases of exercise-induced hyponatremia also increased.

Some sports researchers now suggest drinking only according to thirst during exercise, and this is where we differ a small amount in our approach. There are many valid points to the drink to thirst suggestion, and there are studies showing that those who drink to thirst perform well, even despite some losing more than 2 percent of their body weight (Beis et al, 2012). In addition, in long events, the percent loss of body mass isn't always exactly equivalent to sweat rate – it is also influenced through fuel oxidation and the use of glycogen (which is stored in the muscle with water) which affect fluid balance (Tam et al, 2011). Thus, a loss of x percent of body mass in a very long event does not mean that *all* the fluid was lost through sweat alone.

However, there are several reasons that the 'drink to thirst' strategy may be difficult when used as the *only* guideline for athletes:

1) If you're caught up in the excitement of a race and everything that's going on, you may not be paying attention to your thirst.

2) Depending on your preparation and the distance at which aid stations are spaced, you may not have the ability to always drink to thirst. For example, let's say in previous training sessions you didn't feel as thirsty, so you packed a minimal amount of hydration on the bike or didn't bring a fuel belt for your run. However, today you are experiencing much more thirst, but you don't have hydration with you. This is where things get tricky. The 'drink to thirst' theory assumes that we are carrying enough hydration with us to drink whenever possible, which isn't always the case (particularly in longer races).

3) On average, the level of dehydration when the thirst mechanism kicks in is around a 1 to 2 percent loss in weight. This can vary among individuals, with older athletes experiencing a reduced thirst sensation. If you practice drinking to thirst but commonly lose more than 2 to 3 percent of your body weight during exercise, your thirst mechanism may kick in late and you may not be hydrating enough for optimal performance.

Now, it's obviously important to consider race distance when thinking about these hydration tips. Shorter road races – like a 5K for example – don't warrant much attention to hydration during exercise, aside from satisfying your own thirst. You'll be done before it really makes any difference.

For somewhat longer races, like a sprint distance triathlon, there's not a need to get too crazy about hydration, but you'll want to pay a bit more attention to it and also consider weather conditions. If you'll be out there for one to two hours, swigging some sports drink on the bike and a stop at the aid stations during the run according to thirst will likely take care of your needs. Hotter weather conditions warrant a bit more focus on hydration/electrolytes compared to cooler weather.

For marathoners, and Olympic, Half-Iron, and full Ironman distance triathletes, though, you'll want to develop a personalized hydration plan using what's called a "sweat test," *and* combine this with listening to your body's signals indicating thirst (dry mouth, craving water) or over-drinking (sloshing, bloating, nausea). The International Marathon Medical Director's Association supports the use of a sweat test as a generalized strategy for a fluid plan, combined with deferring to your body's physiologic cues when in question of whether to drink or not (IMMDA, 2006).

The Sweat Test

During a sweat test, you use calculations to figure out how quickly your body loses water via sweat during a long workout. Because people sweat at different rates, this gives you a very individualized and personal way of figuring out your ideal hydration plan.

In a sweat test, you weigh yourself before exercise. You then note how much fluid you are bringing with you for your workout. After the workout, you note how much fluid you ended with and weigh yourself again. The difference in your weight in ounces plus any fluid you consumed, divided by the hours of your workout, is equal to your hourly sweat rate. I have included a sweat test worksheet in the appendix that you can use on your own to determine your needs – it's much easier to understand when you see the formula written out!

If you gained weight during your sweat test, you are drinking too much. If you are within the range of a 2 percent loss of your normal body weight, your hydration rate was probably spot-on. If you lost quite a bit of weight, you likely need to drink more.

Once you know your hourly sweat rate, your goal is to consume enough that you don't lose more than 2 to 3 percent of your body's weight, but also not drink so much that you gain any weight. Again, let the sweat test provide you with a general idea of how much hydration you'll want to carry on the bike, on a fuel belt, or how often you plan to stop at aid stations – but let your body's signals of thirst and over-drinking guide you when in question during training and races.

Aren't there any general recommendations?
If the sweat tests sounds like a bit too much work, and you are nervous about your ability to follow your body's thirst signals, you can consider some general guidelines as a *starting point*.

The ACSM guidelines currently suggest a hydration range of 0.4 to 0.8 liters per hour, as guided by thirst, for marathon runners - which could likely be extrapolated to other types of endurance athletes as well. At the higher end of the range would be athletes who are heavier, faster, or those competing in hot environments. At the lower end of the range would be athletes who are lighter, slower, or those competing in cooler environments.

If we divide this up over the course of an event, and add in some pre/post-race guidelines, the breakdown might look something like the chart on the following page. Again though, please let your individual sweat rate and signs of thirst/overdrinking be your true guide.

General Hydration Estimates:

2 to 4 hours before	5 to 10 ml/kg of water/sports drink – for most athletes, this would be approximately 10-25 ounces
10-15 minutes before	5 to 10 ounces water/sports drink, guided by thirst
Every 15 to 20 minutes of event	3-8 ounces fluid (estimate, guided by thirst) *Preferably develop a generalized plan for individual needs via sweat test* Fluid (or accompanying foods) should have electrolytes in events lasting 1+ hour
After event	Drink 16 to 24 ounces fluid for each pound lost (with electrolytes in the fluid or accompanying food).

*Developed using ACSM, 2007 and Goulet, 2012

You'll notice after the event that there is a range of 16 to 24 ounces recommended for each pound lost. This is to account for the fact that once exercise has ceased, the mechanism for increasing urine production becomes more effective again. In order to properly rehydrate, some individuals may need slightly more than the pound equivalent (16 ounces = 1 pound) of hydration. Consuming fluid over time after the event (rather than all at once immediately after) and consuming it with electrolytes (whether in the beverage itself or through normal food intake) helps to properly rehydrate (ACSM, 2007).

Remember, you want to try to nail down your ideal race day strategies during training, so practice your hydration and fueling needs throughout your training season to determine what your optimal amounts are. And above all, if you feel a sloshing in your stomach or nausea, and you've been drinking a lot of water, stop drinking for a bit. Hyponatremia is inherently more dangerous and life threatening than a case of mild dehydration, despite the more common prevalence of dehydration.

TL;DR Tips on Hydration

- Use a personalized hydration plan guided by sweat test results (use the worksheet in the appendix) and thirst.
- Keep sweat losses to less than 2 to 3 percent of your body weight.
- Listen to your body's signals for guidance to drink more (dry mouth, craving water) or drink less (sloshing, nausea).
- If you are experiencing nausea, vomiting, and disorientation on the course, you may want to ask for a medic in case of hyponatremia.

Electrolytes for Exercise

In addition to the fluid lost through sweating, sweat also contains electrolytes. Though there are several electrolytes lost in sweat, we are most concerned about sodium. Athletes who participate in long distance triathlons or ultra-marathons may also be concerned about potassium.

Potassium

Athletes often ask if they should be concerned about potassium losses. Potassium is important for heart health and muscular contractions, and we should aim to get the recommended amount of potassium each day through our regular food intake. During exercise, you do lose a small amount of potassium through sweat. However, athletes typically don't need worry about replenishing these losses in any special way during exercise lasting only a few hours (Mahan et al, 2012). Most sports and electrolyte drinks or products contain small amounts of potassium that are plenty adequate for potassium losses.

Athletes participating in long distance or ultra events – particularly those drinking water and eating a non-potassium-rich food – may want to add in a potassium rich food or a sports beverage to their fueling plan. In these cases, the losses through sweat could be significant over several hours to warrant the additional potassium – but it doesn't need to be in mega-doses.

Though newer research suggests muscle cramping is more due to neuromuscular fatigue rather than potassium losses, there is of course anecdotal evidence from runners and coaches who feel a lack of potassium during exercise contributes to cramps. If you feel like a potassium-rich banana on a long run will be beneficial, then by all means eat up.

I strongly advise against taking high-dose potassium supplement pills during exercise (unless a doctor has advised you to). This is because potassium losses are not that high during exercise, and too much potassium can actually lead to dangerous electrolyte imbalances and irregular heart rhythms.

Please note that standard electrolyte pills or tabs designed for endurance exercise that contain a small amount of potassium are completely fine. I am referring instead to the high-dose potassium-only supplements that can sometimes be found at vitamin stores or online.

Spotlight on Sodium

The most important electrolyte to focus on during training and races is sodium. Sodium is an essential electrolyte that regulates fluid balance and plays a role in muscle and nerve function. Though too much sodium on an everyday basis can potentially affect blood pressure, it's actually quite important for athletes to make sure they are getting enough during exercise. Losing too much sodium during an event may put you at greater risk for issues like heat cramping or early fatigue. Though much of the evidence on cramping and sodium is anecdotal, many sports dietitians have had "heavy salt sweaters" – clients who lose a lot of sodium in their sweat – see success with decreased cramping when they upped their sodium intake during long sessions. In addition, sodium helps to stimulate our thirst mechanism, leading us to maintain better hydration levels.

A lack of sodium may also increase the risk of hyponatremia (that dangerous drop in blood sodium levels discussed in the hydration section). While fluid overload is the primary factor causing hyponatremia, a lack of sodium intake may play a role as well. And research shows that consuming foods or beverages with sodium during exercise helps to maintain plasma sodium levels better compared to water alone (Baker et al, 2008; Anastasiou et al, 2009).

So is this a license for us to load up on pepperoni pizza and Big Macs every day in the name of sodium for athletic performance? Of course not (as much as some of us might enjoy that)! The key to sodium balance for athletes is to consume additional sodium when it is actually needed, which is during exercise.

How much sodium should I take in during exercise?
It's actually a bit difficult to make a general recommendation for sodium intake during exercise, since sweat losses vary greatly. The rate that you sweat, and how much sodium is in that sweat, is influenced by factors like genetics, body weight, heat acclimatization, and the intensity of exercise.

As a starting point, the ACSM recommends 500 to 700 mg of sodium per liter of fluid you drink during exercise that lasts more than an hour. Most commercial sports drinks provide 110 to 170 mg of sodium per 8 ounces (a little less than 0.25 liters), which will do the trick for replenishing sodium around this rate (464 to 718 mg per liter at this range). You can also use commercial sports products (like gels or blocks) or real foods that contain sodium (note – not all of them do, and some contain low amounts), and hydrate with water.

If you're a heavy salt sweater or you're exercising in the heat, you may need somewhat higher amounts of sodium. This is particularly true if you're not acclimated to the heat, as you lose a higher overall amount of sodium at a given sweat rate when you are not used to performing in the heat (Buono et al, 2007).

Keep in mind the distance of a race as well. A sprint distance race probably doesn't require much worrying about sodium aside from a few swigs of a sports drink on the bike, as it is short (aka less time sweating) and you can easily replenish losses with a post-race meal.

Of course, if it's very hot outside or you are a slower athlete, you may need to focus on taking in a bit more sodium.

However, in longer events, there is a greater potential for fluid, electrolyte, and fuel mismatches. Events longer than four hours may require higher amounts of sodium than the general recommendation.

If you fall into one of the categories that may require additional sodium (either at the higher end of the ACSM range or perhaps even above that range), consider the following options for increasing sodium intake during exercise:

- Use a higher sodium sports drink product. For example, the Ironman Perform Drink contains 190 mg of sodium in 8 ounces, versus 110 to 120 mg of sodium in the same amount of other common sports drinks.
- Add an extra 1/8 teaspoon of salt to your normal sports drink.
- Try real foods that are high in sodium during the bike portion. Ideas include pretzels, beef jerky, or V8.
- If you need more sodium than the above options (perhaps you're eating a low sodium carbohydrate food and hydrating with water, for example) then consider a salt/electrolyte tablet.

Experiment with fluid and sodium needs during training to develop a plan that works for you!

TL;DR Tips on Electrolytes

- Sodium is the most important electrolyte to worry about during exercise.
- Consume beverages or foods that contain sodium during exercise lasting over an hour.
- Try to acclimatize to the heat if you will be racing in it.

- You may need more sodium than the amount in a standard sports drink if you are a heavy salt sweater, the race weather is hot, and/or if you are exercising for more than a few hours.
- Experiment with sodium intake during training to develop a plan for race day.

Pre-Exercise Meals

Pre-Exercise Meals

Now it's time to move forward into figuring out fueling needs. Let's start with pre-exercise meals, which apply to meals both before a long training day as well as those before a race.

A meal before exercise serves many purposes. First off, it's going to help fuel your muscles. The carbohydrate in that meal will be available as an energy source. This carbohydrate also helps to prevent low blood sugar, which can sometimes be a problem for morning exercisers who go out for a training session on an empty stomach. A pre-exercise meal also helps (as simple as this seems) to prevent hunger during your workout. For a short training session this isn't a huge concern, but if you will be doing a 20 mile training run or you're about to embark on a 70.3 triathlon, you don't want to arrive at the start feeling ravenous. It can be hard to push yourself when all you're thinking about is your next chance to have a meal.

What should I eat before exercising?

A pre-exercise meal should provide your body with carbohydrates to fuel your muscles. The composition of the pre-exercise meal, including the number of carbohydrates and the other components of the meal, depends on how far in advance you are eating. The further out from the training session or race, the more food you'll need to eat, but you'll also have more flexibility with the types of food since you have more time for digestion. If you eat closer to a training session or race, you'll need to eat less and you'll need to choose easily digested foods because your body doesn't have as much time to process it. You don't want to feel too full (or even worse, bloated/nauseous) going out to swim, ride, or run!

Keep in mind that these guidelines for pre-exercise meals apply to moderate to intense exercise lasting more than an hour, or very intense sessions that are slightly shorter than this. If you're going out for a 30 minute comfortably paced run, for example, you don't need to worry heavily about these guidelines. In those cases, you can eat a regular meal several hours beforehand or grab a quick snack a little while before hitting the pavement. Whatever works best for you. Short workouts don't require as much forethought. However, for longer workouts or intense sessions, your body will want that pre-exercise fuel.

Below is a chart with guidelines for pre-exercise fueling. The general rule of thumb is 1 gram of carbohydrate per kilogram of body weight, multiplied by the number of hours before the training session/race. As with all parts of sports nutrition, you'll want to experiment with the different strategies and see what works best for you.

Pre-Exercise Fueling Guidelines:

Time frame before training/race	Guidelines
3-4 hours before	3 to 4 g carbohyrate/kg Moderate protein, avoid too much fat/fiber
2-3 hours before	2 to 3 g carbohyrate/kg Moderate protein, low in fat/fiber
1 hour before	1 g carbohyrate/kg Easy to digest, low in fat/fiber
"I hate eating before training/races"	Bigger dinner the night before; sports drink, gel, or carbohydrate-rich snack a few minutes before heading out

*Developed using information from AND (2013) and ACSM/ADA Position Stand, 2007

Based on the athletes I've worked with, many have had the most success either eating around three hours in advance, or eating one hour in advance. For triathletes and runners, many tend to prefer eating one hour in advance since most train and race in the morning. The specific strategy you choose should be one that sits well in your stomach, helps you feel energized throughout your exercise session, and is a comfortable amount of food to eat.

Let's look at an example. Jen is a 150 pound athlete who is debating between eating around three and a half hours before exercise or around one hour before exercise. We take 150 pounds and divide by 2.2 to determine her weight in kilograms = 68 kilograms.

3-4 hours before = 3 to 4 grams carbohydrate/kg
- 4 grams x 68 kilograms = 270 grams carbohydrate
- 3 grams x 68 kilograms = 205 grams carbohydrate

1 hour before = 1 gram/kg
- 1 gram x 68 kilograms = 68 grams

If Jen were eating three and a half hours before, she'd want to aim for 205 to 270 grams of carbohydrate. If she were eating one hour before, she'd aim for around 68 grams of carbohydrate. The chart on the next page shows what the meals from each of these scenarios could look like.

3.5 hours before – Goal is about 230g carbohydrate (mid-range of 205 to 270 grams)	1 hour before – Goal is about 68 g carbohydrate
Meal Example #1: Large plain bagel (65 g) 1 tbsp peanut butter (3 g) 2 tbsp strawberry jam (30 g) Tall (16 ounce) glass of OJ (52 g) Blueberry muffin (80 g) *Total = 230 g*	Meal Example #1: One cup of most cereals (About 25 g) And 1 cup of milk (12 g) With a sliced large banana (30 g) *Total = 67 grams*
Meal Example #2: 1 cup dry rolled oats (60 grams) Cooked with 1 cup water and 1 cup milk (12 grams) With ½ cup raisins (60 grams) And ¼ cup sweetened shredded coconut (11 grams) 1 sliced apple (25 grams) Tall (16 ounce) glass of OJ (52 g) *Total = 220 grams*	Meal Example #2: Large plain bagel (65 g) 1 tbsp peanut butter (3 g) *Total = 68 grams*

You can see the meal examples for three and a half hours beforehand have a considerable amount of food. Some athletes enjoy getting up early and having a big meal far in advance with adequate time to digest. Or, perhaps you have a long training session in the afternoon or evening, and you may be eating several hours in advance at lunch. It'd be important to get a good dose of healthy carbohydrates at that meal.

On the other hand, a lot of athletes tend to train in the mornings and don't want to get up several hours in advance. Many athletes have success with food an hour or so before a long training session or race in the morning. Still, some may not like eating so close to exercising because it gives them a nervous stomach or gastrointestinal upset. It's best to experiment with what works for your body.

To fiber, or not to fiber…

I mentioned this back in the section on carbohydrates, but it's worth repeating. Some athletes are very sensitive to the effects of fiber on their digestive system. Fiber helps keep us "regular," and physical activity also keeps food moving through the digestive system. Too much fiber combined with physical activity (particularly running, as there is more jostling) can result in a rush to the nearest porta-potty.

Consider what you are choosing for a pre-exercise meal based on how far in advance you are eating, the length of your training sessions, and your body's response. If you know that your bowl of oatmeal and raisins fuels you well before exercise and you've never had an issue with diarrhea, then sticking with that is fine. However, if whole grains send you running for the bathroom two hours later, you may want to choose a refined grain (due to the lower fiber content) on the mornings of long training sessions and races.

TL;DR Tips on Pre-Exercise Meals

- Fiber, protein, and fat help you stay full longer, which may or may not be a welcomed side effect for long sessions.
- The further in advance you are eating, the more flexibility you have with the amount of fiber, fat, and protein (meaning you may be able to enjoy moderate to low amounts of foods with these components several hours in advance, but not an hour before the race)
- The shorter and less intense the training session, the less you have to worry about the specific pre-exercise meal composition.

133

- Practice with different timing strategies during training to see what works best for you, as anywhere from one to four hours in advance may be ideal for you.

The Breakfast Conundrum

For many athletes, the pre-exercise meal before a long workout or race is going to be breakfast. Many of these same athletes are already pressed for time, fitting in training among work, family, and other commitments. If you're waking up early on a Sunday to head out for a long run or ride, you may be reluctant to eat anything beforehand for the simple reason that you don't want to wake up earlier. Along the same lines, perhaps you are rushing out the door to go to work in the morning, and figure you'll just wait to eat your calories until lunchtime. However, as the saying goes, breakfast is the most important meal of the day!

Why bother eating breakfast?
Let's start with the basics - skipping breakfast can lead to a shorter attention span, irritability, longer reaction time, and less energy. If you're trying to lose weight, skipping breakfast is not a good idea either. Many people skip breakfast in an attempt to "save" calories for the rest of the day. This often ends up backfiring. You become fatigued and hungry by mid-morning, and this increases your chances of making unhealthy food choices throughout the day. People who skip breakfast often end up overeating at lunch and dinner. In fact, studies of those who have lost weight and successfully kept it off long term show that the majority of these people regularly eat breakfast.

Skipping breakfast may also interfere with your workout routine – if you normally workout during the morning or afternoon, you may feel too tired to exercise. If you work out in the evening, you may feel overly full from overeating at dinnertime, leading to a skipped workout.

Are there any other reasons specific to athletes?
Specifically for runners and triathletes, I want to expand a little bit on the concept of pre-exercise fueling for morning workouts related to the point I mentioned earlier – the meal's importance in

preventing low blood sugar. As we've learned already, your body stores glycogen in your muscles for fuel. It's important to note that your body also stores a very small amount of glycogen in your liver. When your blood sugar levels drop, your liver releases some of this to maintain proper levels.

Overnight, when you're sleeping (and not eating), your body maintains blood sugar levels in a healthy range by using some of that liver glycogen. When you wake up, a good portion of those liver glycogen stores have been depleted.

Here's the issue when it comes to exercise: When you don't eat anything before a workout, you don't provide external sources of sugar to maintain that blood sugar. This means that the liver has to continue to break down glycogen throughout your workout to maintain your blood sugar. Depending on how depleted your glycogen stores are from the night before, eventually during your workout those liver stores can run low. This can make it difficult to maintain proper blood sugar levels.

What happens in these cases if you can't maintain optimal blood sugar levels? You can feel lightheaded and woozy, and you won't be able to push yourself. Not a good place to be in during a training session or (especially) a race.

This is of course a bigger issue for long workouts, bricks (biking training session followed immediately by a run), and races since you're exercising for a longer period of time. If you wake up and plan to do a 30 minute run but hate eating beforehand, there's probably nothing wrong with that as long as a) you feel good during the workout, and b) you eat breakfast at some point afterward. However, if you have a two hour bike/30 minute run brick planned this weekend, you're going to want to seriously consider eating beforehand to fuel your muscles and prevent that blood sugar drop.

Troubleshooting common breakfast problems

"I'm not hungry."
You may be eating too much late at night, which causes you to be less hungry in the morning. It's a good idea to avoid mindless snacking at night, especially on not-so-healthy items. Also, sometimes people just don't feel hungry first thing in the morning, despite not eating late at night. If this is the case and you're not working out first thing in the morning, that's fine – just wait an hour or two and then have your breakfast. Or if you are working out, maybe you eat a small snack before your workout, and then have the rest of your breakfast afterwards.

"I don't like breakfast foods."
No problem. No one says you have to eat breakfast foods in the morning. Any healthy food choice will do!

"I never have enough time."
Prepare your breakfast the night before so it's ready when you are running out the door, or get up a few minutes earlier to make sure you give yourself enough time to eat. Or, try quick grab-and-go options like a piece of fruit & string cheese or nuts. While this might not be as balanced as a sit-down meal, it's certainly better than nothing.

"I can never think of what to make for breakfast."
Check out the quick and easy options on the chart on the following page. Keep in mind the composition of your meal should depend on your workout schedule. If you're eating breakfast an hour before your workout, for example, you'll want to eat a smaller meal with less fat, like a small bowl of cereal with skim milk and a banana. If it's a rest day or you're working out later in the afternoon/evening, you could eat a larger meal that's more flexible in fat/protein/fiber content – perhaps a breakfast burrito on a whole wheat wrap.

Quick & Easy Breakfast Ideas:

At home:	On-the-go:
Cereal and milk with a piece of fruit	Fruit and string cheese
Peanut butter or almond butter on whole wheat toast/bagels/English muffins	Fruit and ½ to 1 ounce nuts (almonds, pecans, walnuts)
Breakfast burrito: Scrambled eggs (you can microwave if you don't have time to cook on the stovetop) in a whole wheat burrito with salsa	Turkey and cheese sandwich on whole wheat bread (made the night before)
Whole grain waffle or pancakes topped with fruit	Homemade whole grain muffins (made on the weekend) and a piece of fruit
Yogurt with fruit and granola	Larabars
Smoothies (fruit, milk/yogurt, spinach, flax, protein powder, etc. – so many options!)	Applesauce "squeeze" packages and string cheese or a hardboiled egg
Oatmeal with fresh or dried fruit and nuts	Fast food takeout: • Whole wheat bagel with light cream cheese or peanut butter • Oatmeal with dried fruit toppings • Ham, egg and cheese on an English Muffin

Cereal? For adults?

You may notice that cereal is mentioned a few times in this book –
in the previous chart as well as our pre-exercise meal examples.
And this is for good reason. It's easy, cheap, practical, and quick to
throw together. Plus, cereal, milk and fruit as a meal provides three
different food groups and a variety of nutrients. Nancy Clark,
another leading sports dietitian, promotes cereal as a good option
in many of her books and to her clients, and I definitely agree with
her.

There are a few steps you can take to make sure you choose a
healthy cereal at breakfast:

1) Check the *sugar*. While opinions vary among dietitians about
the upper limit for sugar per serving in cereals, I generally
recommend that people stick to those with less than 6 grams per
serving. One exception to the 6 gram of sugar rule is if you are
eating a cereal that contains dried fruit. Dried fruit is a
concentrated source of natural sugar, so it does boost the sugar
content but also contributes many other nutrients. Also, if the
cereal contains more than 7 or 8 grams of natural fiber, you can get
away with a slightly higher amount of sugar per serving.

2) Check the ingredient label and be sure you see a *whole grain* as
the first ingredient. Look for words like "whole grain oats," "whole
wheat," "whole grain corn," etc.   And remember that "multigrain"
is an unregulated term – a cereal can be labeled "multigrain" but
not contain any whole grains.

3) Find the *fiber*. As a minimum, you want your cereal to have at
least 2 to 3 grams of fiber. Amounts in this range are fine to eat pre-
exercise and shouldn't cause any gastrointestinal upset. For
breakfasts on non-training days or afternoon/evening training
sessions, or if you aren't sensitive to the effects of fiber pre-exercise,
you should look for cereals with higher amounts.

Some healthy options that meet the criteria above would include Cheerios, Multigrain Cheerios, Life, Kashi Go Lean Original, Wheaties, Kix, Total, or Barbara's Shredded Spoonful's Multigrain. There are plenty more out there – just check the labels!

But I still don't want to eat breakfast!
If you absolutely hate eating breakfast, try to have a mid-morning snack to avoid being ravenous by lunch time. And be sure that before a longer workout, you follow these next-best tips: 1) eat an adequate dinner rich in carbohydrates the night before, and 2) then have a carbohydrate-rich snack, take a gel, or sip some sports drink a few minutes before going out. The dinner the night before helps to top off your muscle glycogen stores, and the snack/gel/sports drink in the morning helps to ensure you have some external carbohydrate coming in to maintain blood sugar levels.

Race Day Considerations
Whatever strategy you decide works best for you, remember to stick with that on race day. Choose familiar foods that you eat often and that you know sit well in your stomach. This isn't the time to be an adventurous eater – there are plenty of other days for that!

Along the same lines, if you normally eat one hour before training, don't eat five hours beforehand on the day of your big event (you'll likely underfuel and be tired during the race). Keep in mind the start time of the race when considering this. I have one client, for example, that always ate breakfast around 8AM and did her training sessions at 9AM. On the morning of her half marathon, she ate at the same time – 8AM – but the race didn't start until 11AM. She ended up feeling exhausted during it. When she adjusted her breakfast timing before subsequent races to more closely reflect the timing of her training breakfasts, she felt much better.

TL;DR Tips on Breakfast

- Pre-exercise breakfast helps maintain blood sugar levels and may assist in weight loss efforts.
- Stick with familiar foods and timing on your race day breakfast.
- If you absolutely hate eating before long workouts/races, be sure to have a carb-rich dinner the night before, and eat a snack, take a gel, or sip some sports drink a few minutes before heading out.

Rebound hypoglycemia

This is a condition that occurs in some individuals when they eat before working out and experience a drop in blood sugar levels. This can lead to that same lightheaded, woozy feeling I described when you skip a pre-exercise meal/snack. In this case, though, the person ate beforehand. So, what happened?

The issue is often with timing. There is a "risky window" about 20 to 45 minutes before exercise. The person will eat something, but the body starts the digestive process and insulin secretion before exercise begins. Insulin's job is to move sugar out of the blood and into cells. This, combined with the natural blood sugar lowering effect of exercise itself, causes too large a drop in blood sugar levels and that lightheaded effect.

If you struggle with rebound hypoglycemia, there are a few tips I can give you:

1) Avoid eating in the "risky window" of 20 to 45 minutes before a workout

2) Eat at least one hour in advance or sip a sports drink/eat a snack 5-10 minutes before starting exercise. The latter option doesn't give your body enough time to secrete insulin, and the insulin response is somewhat inhibited once you start exercise – meaning that snack will help to maintain your blood sugar levels and prevent a drop.

3) Experiment with the type of foods you eat. Some athletes may need to eat further out and have a more slowly digesting carbohydrate source, while others may be fine with a quicker-digesting choice as long as it's at least one hour in advance.

4) If you are feeling lightheaded during a workout and are afraid you may pass out, stop and eat or drink a carbohydrate-containing snack/beverage.

5) If you struggle with rebound hypoglycemia, you may want to carry snacks or a beverage with you even on shorter training sessions (those less than one hour).

Glycemic index – is it useful for pre-exercise meals?

Glycemic index (or GI) refers to how quickly a food raises your blood sugar and, consequently, your insulin levels as they increase to account for the spike in blood sugar. Certain foods cause a higher and quicker spike in blood sugar compared to others. The glycemic index is not as clear cut as complex carbohydrates and simple sugars, though. It is affected by many factors, including (Gonzalez et al, 2012; Mondazzi et al, 2009):

- Ripeness of produce, as fruits and vegetables that are more ripe typically have a higher concentration of sugar versus starch, which leads to a higher glycemic index
- The amount of fiber in food, which helps to slow digestion and leads to a slower, prolonged release of sugar into the blood stream
- The form of food, including whether something is finely ground versus coarsely ground; the way it is cooked (al dente pasta, for example, has a lower glycemic index compared to softer pasta); liquids versus solids; etc.
- Type of carbohydrates – starches like that in potatoes are absorbed more rapidly than other types of starches
- The amount of protein and fat, both of which slow digestion and drop the glycemic index of the food

The chart on the following page gives some examples of foods that are categorized as high GI, moderate GI, and low GI. The GI numerical value is in comparison to a standard dose of glucose, which gives a GI value of 100.

Glycemic Index of Common Foods

High GI foods	>70	bagels, pancakes, waffles, white bread, potato, cornflakes cereal, Gatorade, instant flavored oatmeal packets, rice cakes, watermelon
Moderate GI foods	55-70	pineapple, muesli, shredded wheat cereal, bran flakes cereal, blueberry muffin, oatmeal from rolled oats, couscous, banana, kiwi, raisins, popcorn
Low GI foods	<55	barley, yogurt, beans, lentils, apples, oranges, spaghetti, smoothies (made with milk and fruit), oatmeal from steel cut oats, All-Bran cereal, milk, dried apricots, peaches, apple juice, nuts, vegetable soup, non-starchy vegetables

*Developed using Atkinson et al, 2008

Glycemic index and overall health for athletes

On an everyday basis, from a metabolic health standpoint, we want to avoid giant spikes and drops in blood sugar levels. Eating a diet with too many high glycemic index choices can cause large swings in sugar/insulin levels and has been associated with an increased risk of certain health conditions including obesity, elevated triglycerides, and metabolic syndrome (Finley et al, 2010).

However, the glycemic index can be an overwhelming tool to use with daily nutrition, and may not be practical for athletes for several reasons:

- Your body's individual glycemic response can vary as much as 43 percent over the course of the day (Vega-Lopez, 2007).

145

- When high GI foods are combined with other types of foods, it can alter the impact on your blood glucose (which happens often, since many of us eat more than one type of food during a meal or snack). For example, eating a bagel with peanut butter and a glass of milk will cause a slower rise in blood sugar compared to the bagel alone.
- Portions of a food are going to influence how much blood glucose rises. If you only eat a few bites of a high GI food, it won't raise your blood sugar levels as much as a large portion.
- Foods that fall into the high GI range can still be healthy for us to eat (watermelon, for example!).
- Athletes may have differences in glycemic index responses compared to sedentary individuals (Mettler et al, 2007). Athletes tend to have improved insulin sensitivity, meaning it doesn't take as much insulin to lower blood sugar for a certain amount of carbohydrate, compared to the amount it would take in a sedentary person.

From my standpoint, it's easier to simply focus on an overall balanced diet that's high in fruits, vegetables, whole grains, and other plant based foods along with moderate protein (from lean meats/plant proteins) and healthy fats. Along the same lines, avoid overly processed foods and refined grains most of the time. By following these simple guidelines, you'll optimize your health without having to worry about glycemic index consistently, and you'll likely be choosing a variety of low to moderate glycemic index foods on an everyday basis anyway.

Glycemic index and pre-exercise meals:
Now, with regards to endurance exercise fueling, scientific theories have suggested that glycemic index may be important to consider with regards to pre-exercise meals. Unfortunately, these theories aren't supported by much proof or practicality.

The main theory is that pre-race meals comprised of low GI choices would be better for athletes, as they would lead to a more sustained release of energy, along with better blood sugar control and less insulin released during exercise. Insulin is an inhibitor of lipolysis (meaning fat breakdown), which means that higher insulin levels may theoretically create a heavier reliance on carbohydrate utilization during exercise. Thus, a low GI meal would lead to less of an insulin spike, in turn shifting your body towards use of a higher percentage of fat for fuel, and decreasing the reliance on carbohydrate and improving endurance performance.

There have been a considerable number of studies done on this topic, but results vary. There's really nothing to definitively support this theory or improved performance using low GI meals before exercise. Taken as a whole, the research seems to lean towards equal performance comparing low GI to high GI meals. If you're interested in the particular studies, here's a quick summary of research from the last several years:

Beneficial effect of low GI pre-exercise meal on performance:
- *Moore et al (2013):* In untrained females, a low GI meal two hours before exercise led to better cycling time trial performance compared to a high GI meal (67 vs 49 minutes).

- *Moore et al (2010):* 40 kilometer time trial performance was better among 10 male cyclists after a low GI meal compared to a high GI meal (96 minutes versus 93 minutes).

- *Moore et al (2009):* When eight cyclists completed a 40 kilometer time trial after eating either a low GI or high GI meal on different occasions, their performance was better after the low GI meal (95.6 versus 92.5 minutes).

- *Wu et al (2008):* When eight recreational male runners ate either a high GI or a low GI meal three hours before exercising, they were able run longer after the lower GI meal (109 versus 101 minutes).

No effect of low GI pre-exercise meal on performance:
- *Bennett et al (2012):* A low GI meal eaten two hours before exercise did improve metabolic outcomes (less of a spike in blood glucose before exercise and lower carbohydrate oxidation at the start of exercise) compared to a high GI meal, but did not affect performance during 90-minute intermittent high-intensity treadmill running sessions.

- *Karamanolis et al (2011):* Runners who ate a low GI meal before performing a treadmill endurance test had a better metabolic profile in terms of glycemic control, but had no difference in performance.

- *Little et al (2010):* GI did not affect the type of substrate utilization (the percentages of carbohydrate and fat used) among male athletes in 90-min high-intensity intermittent running trials, nor did it affect their blood glucose levels during exercise.

- *Moore et al (2009):* For nine male athletes completing several 21 kilometer running trials, a low GI meal resulted in differences in pre-exercise blood glucose and insulin levels, but did not lead to a difference in substrate utilization (carbohydrate versus fat) and also did not lead to better performance.

- *Hamzah et al (2009):* This study looked at glycemic intake over a longer period. Participants either ate a control (regular) diet, a high GI diet, or a low GI diet – all over a five day period each. After the five days, they completed a treadmill run to exhaustion. There were no differences in substrate utilization or performance between the low GI and high GI diets.

- *Chen et al (2009):* When researchers compared a pre-exercise, low GI meal to a pre-exercise high GI meal among eight males completing a 21 kilometer time trial, they found no difference in performance.

- *Chen et al (2008):* Eight male runners completed several trials of a one hour run followed by a 10 kilometer time trial. Two hours before the different trials, they ate either a high GI meal, a low GI meal, or a control meal. There was no difference in 10 kilometer time trial performance between the high GI or low GI meals.

It seems that as long as carbohydrate sources are consumed during the exercise sessions lasting one hour or more, there is no performance benefit from eating a low glycemic index meal beforehand compared to a high GI meal.

In addition, it may be difficult to create a low-GI meal that is palatable for a breakfast choice and still provides adequate carbohydrate. Plus, many low-GI foods are higher in fiber, which could lead to gastrointestinal upset during exercise.

A low GI meal before exercise may improve metabolic control and stabilize blood sugar better, though, which could be of interest to athletes struggling with elevated cholesterol levels or metabolic syndrome.

I recommend that you choose a pre-exercise meal that is rich in carbohydrates (following the guidelines suggested in this book) and simply eat what feels right and seems to provide you with the best energy for your training. You can always experiment with whether a low GI meal or a high GI meal works better for you before long workouts/races – but don't force yourself to scarf down a bowl of beans and lentils before a race simply because they're low GI! If a high GI meal is easier on the stomach and you feel good during training, use that. If a low GI meal seems to give you a more sustained energy, then use that.

TL;DR Tips on Glycemic Index & Pre-Exercise Meals

- Glycemic index (GI) refers to your blood sugar response after eating a certain food.
- GI varies based on many factors, including those of the food(s) and among each person. It is not a clear-cut science.
- Low GI meals may be advantageous for athletes struggling with high cholesterol levels.
- On the whole, research does not currently support a performance benefit to eating low GI meals in pre-exercise meals.
- Many low GI foods are higher in fiber, which may contribute to gastrointestinal upset during exercise.
- Your pre-exercise meal should be based on palatability, gastrointestinal comfort, and perceived energy levels during training. Practice with what works best for you, whether that's a low GI or high GI meal.

Carbohydrate Loading

A discussion of pre-exercise meals wouldn't be complete without a section on carbohydrate loading. Carbohydrate loading refers to the strategy of eating high carbohydrate meals in the days leading up to the race, and is beneficial when you will be competing in events lasting longer than 90 minutes. In fact, research shows carbohydrate loading may result in up to a 20 percent longer time until fatigue in endurance events (Hawley et al, 1997).

Why carbohydrate load?

Let's imagine a sponge. You put it under the sink for a few seconds with the sink turned on super low, like at a drip-drop pace. The sponge is still dry in some places and only slightly saturated in others. Now, squeeze the sponge. Not much water comes out right?

Imagine the same sponge, but you have completely saturated it with water. When you go to squeeze it, you are able to squeeze out a large amount of water.

This is comparable to fueling properly in the days leading up to a race. If you only eat minimal amounts of carbohydrate, you are not putting enough energy in your muscles. When your muscles begin working in the race, the glycogen supply will run out quickly. On the other hand, if you eat properly in the few days leading up to the race, you fully saturate your muscles (like that sponge) with all the glycogen that it can hold. This means you will be as prepared as possible at the starting line.

How much should I eat leading up to the race?

While many people envision carb-loading as stuffing themselves with as much pasta as possible, this is not the case. Actually, if you are eating a proper athletic diet that is rich in healthy carbohydrates (amount based on your training, as described earlier in the section on carbohydrates), you won't have to alter your eating plan too much in the week leading up to the race. The reason? Tapering!

If you are tapering your workouts the way most coaches recommend, with a 2-3 week decrease in training volume, you are burning less calories – and using less glycogen - throughout those weeks. So, if you continue eating the proportion of carbohydrate in your normal training diet, you are essentially carb-loading just by doing that! The proportion of carbohydrate you're eating compared to what you're burning is now greater (since you're burning less), so you are able to saturate those muscles with glycogen in advance of your race.

Thus, there is no need to spend every waking moment consuming carbohydrate leading up to a race. However, you should make an effort to continue your normal training diet that's rich in carbohydrate choices. And in the two to three days before your race, you can slightly increase your carbohydrate intake (up to approximately 70 percent of your daily calories) to ensure your muscles are fully stocked with glycogen (Rauch et al, 1995; Chen et al, 2008).

A few more tips:
- Choose familiar foods. Even though you may be excited about a pre-race party the night before, try to avoid reaching for new items or those that you don't eat often. They may settle heavily in your stomach, or cause problems like diarrhea.
- Pasta isn't the only choice. You can carb-load on a combination of rice, pancakes, quinoa, potatoes, starchy vegetables, fruits, and more. The type of carbohydrate is not as important as the amount (Chen et al, 2008).
- In addition, using a variety of familiar foods is best practice because you decrease the risk of overdoing any one food. For example, carb-loading on fruit alone may result in

diarrhea, while carb-loading on white bread alone may cause constipation in the days leading up to the race.

- You may end up with a "nervous stomach" the night before a race, making it even more important that you eat a carb-rich meal two nights beforehand. Along the same lines, if dinner usually doesn't sit well before a race, try a large lunch the day before instead.
- If you've carb-loaded correctly, you may notice a few pounds gained on the scale. When your body stores carbohydrate as glycogen in your muscles, it stores it with water. This is normal, and will not hurt your performance. it will actually be beneficial, as you know that your muscles are energy-loaded and ready to work!

TL;DR Tips on Carbohydrate Loading

- Carbohydrate loading is beneficial for events lasting longer than 90 minutes.
- Eating your normal training diet during tapering, along with slightly increasing carbohydrate intake during the three days before the race (about 70 percent of calories), can be a successful strategy for carb-loading.

Fueling During Exercise

Fueling During Exercise

This is the topic that runners and triathletes tend to feel most confused about. Questions I hear often include: "What is the best product to take in during a race? Should I use gels, shot blocks, sports beans, or real food? How much do I need? Should I combine this with a sports drink? How do I eat without my stomach hurting?"

Any of these concerns sound familiar to you? If so, you are not alone. Nailing down a proper race day fueling plan can be tough because a) sometimes people aren't familiar with sports nutrition recommendations, b) there are so many sources of information out there that it can be hard sifting through them all to find accurate information, and c) every person's body is different, so a fueling plan that works for one individual may not work for another.

I'm going to give you some great guidelines in this section, but if I can present you with one take home point, it is this: After you figure out a sample fueling plan based on these guidelines, practice during training! Your race-day fueling plan should not be something new. You should experiment with fueling plans during training to nail down the one best plan that seems to consistently give you energy and that your gastrointestinal system tolerates well. Just like you have to train your muscles to run, bike, and swim, you have to train your gut to get used to taking in food during exercise.

Why fuel during exercise?

You may be wondering why it is even important to fuel yourself during exercise, and that is a valid point. In fact, sometimes you may not need to worry about fueling during exercise, like if you're working out or racing for a short period of time (an hour or less). However, when you exercise for longer periods of time, your body needs a key nutrient – those carbohydrates – to continue to fuel your muscles.

During exercise, your body has two main sources of energy. In high intensity, short duration exercise, your body relies almost exclusively on carbohydrates stored in your muscles as glycogen. You get a quick turnover of energy that can only be sustained for so long. In moderate intensity, long duration exercise, your body relies on both carbohydrate as well as stores of fat. When you train and race in endurance sports like road races or triathlons, you are always using a mix of these two fuel sources.

Now, in terms of the fat that you burn, your body generally has plenty of that available. In fact, the whole body only stores about 1500 to 2000 calories worth of glycogen in muscles, yet the average athlete has about 50,000 to 100,000 calories worth of energy in stored fat. The problem is that when your muscles run low on glycogen, you can't just shift completely over to fat. You need enough carbohydrate for them to work properly, even in the presence of lots of available fat during moderate intensity exercise. Because of this, it's important to ensure your muscles are saturated with glycogen ahead of time via your everyday training diet, and that you fuel with carbohydrate during exercise to provide continuous fuel.

Let's go back to that sponge analogy I mentioned in an earlier chapter. We talked about how your muscles are like sponges, and we want to have them fully saturated with as much carbohydrate as possible in preparation for a long training day or a big race. Along the same lines, you can only saturate a sponge so much, right? If you keep adding more and more water to a sponge, it won't matter because it can only hold so much before the water will just pass right through or over it. Our muscles are similar because they can only hold so much glycogen. This means it's important for us to consume adequate carbohydrates in the days leading up to a training session or race to make sure our muscles have that maximum amount of glycogen, but it also means we need to fuel our muscles properly during the event by taking in nutrition to supplement these stores.

Also keep in mind - as many of you well know from your training sessions and races - that an exercise that seems to be moderate in intensity (and thus using a mixture of fat and carbohydrate as fuel) can become increasingly difficult as you extend the time frame in which you compete. Even though running a 10 minute mile might be comfortable for you over a 10K distance, when you are running that same 10K at the end of an Olympic Triathlon, your body is tired and keeping that pace certainly feels more difficult. At some point during steady state exercise, your heart rate begins to drift upwards, and it becomes increasingly challenging for your body to maintain that pace. This is termed "cardiac drift." Basically, the amount of blood your heart pumps each time it beats decreases, so your heart has to beat faster to supply your muscles with the blood it needs to meet the metabolic demands of the exercise. You can help prevent cardiac drift to a certain degree (not completely) through proper hydration, electrolyte balance, and maintaining glucose levels by fueling with carbohydrate during exercise.

In addition, once cardiac drift starts to occur, your body shifts towards using an increasingly large proportion of carbohydrate as fuel (as opposed to a relatively equal balance of fat and carbohydrate). Plus, exercise feels harder.

What does all this mean? It means you should take in carbohydrates during training or racing lasting over one hour to help supply your muscles with energy, reduce the risk of excessive cardiac drift, and optimize performance!

In addition, following your training plan is essential for fueling benefits. Not only is consistent training important for improving your speed and endurance, but it also has benefits at the biochemical level. Consistent training increases your body's ability to utilize fat at a given intensity level and increases the ability of your muscles to store glycogen.

So now that you know how important fueling is, the question becomes – how much carbohydrate should you take in, and in what form?

How much carbohydrate?

The amount of carbohydrate needed during exercise varies based on the length of time you will be exercising. The goal is not to replenish every calorie that you are burning – that would actually be a disastrous plan because your body cannot physically absorb that much in a given time frame during exercise. The goal is to simply provide enough to ensure a continuous flow of energy to support the muscles.

Time Frame	Amount of Carbohydrate
Less than 45 minutes	Not needed
45 minutes to 1:15	No physiologic need, but mouth rinse and small amounts of carbohydrate may be beneficial
1:15 to 3 hours	30 to 60 grams per hour
Longer 3 hours	Up to 90 grams per hour

*Developed using ACSM & ADA Position Stand, 2007 and Jeukendrup et al, 2011

What the heck is a mouth rinse?

The "mouth rinse" statement is usually confusing for people, so let me address it. This is actually a super interesting phenomenon. For shorter duration exercise that doesn't physiologically require much carbohydrate, there is still a benefit to a few swigs of a sports drink or even just swishing it inside your mouth. When the sugars touch your tongue, it sends a signal to your brain that fuel is coming and activates areas of the brain involved in motivation and reward. Because of this, your body is able to push itself during

160

those last 15 or 20 minutes even more so than if you had just drank water. This has been shown in experiments with both cyclists and runners and led to improved time trial performance between 2-4 percent depending on the study (Painelli et al, 2010).

The largest effects of mouth rinsing on performance have been seen in research where individuals have fasted before exercise. However, this is not a strategy I would recommend for your upcoming race, because the fasting would likely be much more detrimental to performance compared to the additional 2-4 percent performance gain from mouth rinsing. It might be useful if you forgot to eat breakfast or didn't have time for breakfast occasionally before an intense workout of about one hour.

However, there is the potential that mouth rinsing may be beneficial for some individuals in a well-nourished state (Fares et al, 2011). In fact, one study found that even though the carbohydrate mouth rinse improved mean power to a greater degree for those in a fasting state during cycling, the *highest* mean power output and overall performance was when the individuals were in a fed state (rather than a fasted state) combined with the carbohydrate mouth rinse (Lane et al, 2013).

If you are going to try the mouth rinse technique, you should do so every 10-15 minutes during an event lasting between 45 minutes and an hour and 15 minutes. Events shorter than this may not be long enough for any potential performance benefit to present itself, and events longer than this will require you to actually take in the carbohydrate to supply energy to your muscles.

Why do you need more carbohydrate for events over three hours?
You can see from the chart that once you realize your training or event will last more than approximately one hour, you need to start putting together a carbohydrate intake plan amounting to about 30 to 60 grams per hour. However, if you are going to be exercising

longer than three hours, you may need to increase the amount of carbohydrate you are taking in, up to the level of 90 grams per hour. The longer the event, the greater the importance of fueling, and the greater potential for a large mismatch between what you're putting in your body and your activity level. Taking in more carbohydrate per hour during longer events helps you to exercise comfortably for a longer period of time and reduces your risk of hitting the quintessential "wall" too early in your event.

When should I start consuming carbohydrate? And how often?

When the event is lasting longer than an hour or so and requires fueling, you should plan to start your fueling relatively early - around the 30 to 45 minute mark. If you start fueling before that and do so too aggressively, you risk consuming too much and having an upset stomach early on in the race. If you start later, you risk falling "behind" on the optimal rates you want to achieve. If you try to overcompensate for this later with extra fuel, you can also end up with an upset stomach.

How often you consume carbohydrate within the recommended range of intake will depend on the type of product you're using and your own body's tolerance. Generally, it's better to take in a smaller amount of carbohydrate more frequently compared to a lot all at once each hour. For example, maybe you carry raisins with you and eat a few every 10 minutes. However, if you're using a product like gels, it can be more difficult to space out the intake, as most people don't want to carry half-used gels with them until they are ready to eat the rest. It's more practical to simply eat the entire gel at once. It's important to experiment with which products work best for you and the optimal timing during training.

Because the amount of fuel required is more than many athletes will self-select, you may have better luck during training/racing by setting an alarm on your watch to go off every so often as a reminder to fuel. This can help keep you on track with nutrition and hydration.

How do I know how much I'm taking in each hour?
Sometimes clients ask me "How do I know how much carbohydrate is in my fuel? And how do I know how much I'm getting per hour?" This is a good question. You can look at your products' labels or search online for the nutrition facts, and you should be able to find the grams of carbohydrate listed in a serving size. Once you know how much is in a serving, figure out how many servings you are taking in throughout your exercise session, and multiply the number of servings times the grams of carbohydrate. This will give you the total grams of carbohydrate during your session. You can then take this and divide it by hours to get your rate or carbohydrate intake.

Let's look at an example. John likes to use gels that contain 20 grams of carbohydrate in each packet. He is out on a two hour and 30 minute run. At the 30 minute mark, he takes his first gel and then he continues to take one every half hour (so again at 1:00, 1:30, and 2:00).

We basically ignore that first half hour and look at the fueling rate over the rest of the run. So over the two hours that he was fueling, he took in four gels. Then we do a few simple calculations to figure out the rate of carbohydrate intake:
- 4 gels x 20 grams of carbohydrate in each gel = 80 grams of carbohydrate
- 80 grams of carbohydrate / 2 hours of fueling = 40 grams of carbohydrate/hour

Is this in our goal range of 30-60 grams per hour? Sure is!

When I work with athletes, we'll often put together a chart to map out their fueling plan. This helps them stay organized and know exactly what and how much to eat at what time intervals. For example, a fueling plan for one of my client's long bike rides looked like this:

Time	Fuel/hydration	Grams carbohydrate per hour
0 to 30 minutes	N/A (water as desired)	N/A
30 minutes to 1:30	-6 individual shot blocks (1 package) – ideally spaced out 1 every 10 minutes -Drink water with electrolyte fizz tab per thirst	48 grams
1:30 to 2:30	-Sip 8 oz of Ironman Perform -10 Swedish fish -10 mini pretzels -Drink water with electrolyte fizz tab per thirst	17g +18 g +12 g = 47 grams
2:30 to 3:30	-6 individual shot blocks (1 package) – ideally spaced out 1 every 10 minutes -Drink water with electrolyte fizz tab per thirst	48 grams
3:30 to 4:30	-Sip 8 oz of Ironman Perform -10 Swedish fish -10 mini pretzels -Drink water with electrolyte fizz tab per thirst	17g +18 g +12 g = 47 grams

Of course, some clients may need more fuel, some may want a more 'substantial' food during a ride, and others may need less due to gastrointestinal upset. It's all about finding what works for you.

What types of carbohydrates?

The follow up to the question of amount is, of course, what *types* of carbohydrates to actually take in. To understand the ideal food or product choice, you must first know that our goal is to consume "multiple transportable carbohydrates." This is a long scientific phrase that simply means different types of carbohydrates. Our bodies can only absorb so much of any one type of carbohydrate at a time. However, when we take in different types at once, we are able to absorb a larger overall amount. This is especially important for those of you participating in longer events where you may be taking in up to 90 grams of carbohydrate per hour. In addition, researchers have found that taking in multiple types of carbohydrates increases fluid delivery as well as the body's efficiency in oxidizing fuel, which may help reduce gastrointestinal problems (Jeukendrup, 2010).

Most (but not all) engineered sports products, like sports drinks, gels and shot blocks, are created using these different types of sugars to ensure optimal absorption. In addition, the majority of carbohydrate-rich foods naturally contain a variety of different types of sugars.

Among products that contain multiple transportable carbohydrates, research hasn't shown specific differences in either metabolic activity or performance when evaluating solid foods versus liquids during endurance exercise. Research looking at different types of solid products have also not shown one to be far better than another. For example, one study compared using gels, jellybeans, or a sports drink. They also included a water-only trial. Sixteen men and women cycled for 80 minutes followed by a 10 kilometer time trial on each of the four separate occasions (gel, jellybeans, drink, or water trials). They had the same amount/rate of carbohydrate from each option with the exception of the water option. All three carbohydrate sources – the gels, jellybeans, or drink – were equally effective in improving performance compared to the water only trial (Campbell et al, 2008).

What about "real foods"?

Recently, more and more research has focused on looking at natural food choices as fueling options. Now, we all know that sports products can be a bit pricy at times, especially if you train/race often. I personally find it fascinating that there is mounting evidence supporting equivalent benefits of using "real foods" to train or race. I don't mean that a sports drink or a gel isn't actual food, I just use the term "real food" to refer to things that we might eat regularly in our lives which haven't been specifically engineered for sports performance.

One of the most commonly studied "real food" items has been raisins. A 2012 study looked at the effects of using raisins, chews (shot blocks), or water only during a running activity (Too et al, 2012). It was a small study – just 11 males – but each completed all three nutrition scenarios separated by one week. The running activity consisted of an 80 minute run followed by a 5 kilometer time trial.

Every 20 minutes during exercise, each athlete received raisins or chews at an equal rate of carbohydrate intake. Along with this, there was a steady rate of water consumption.

The results?
- The rate of perceived exertion during running did not differ between the raisins and chews. In other words, the runners *felt* the same with either method of fueling.
- Both the chews and the raisins resulted in a 5 kilometer time trial that was on average one minute faster compared to the water-only trial.
- While there was more reported gastrointestinal distress with any carbohydrate consumption (to be expected when compared to just water intake), the rates were still quite low overall and there was no difference between the chews and the raisins.

This means that raisins led to the same performance as sports chews!

Another study compared raisins to sport beans (Rietschier et al, 2011). On separate days, ten male athletes completed two tests each consisting of 120 minutes of constant intensity cycling followed by a 10 kilometer time trial. During each, they received either sport beans or raisins. The amount of calories from each was the same, and they were both given at 20 minute intervals. There were no differences between the sport beans and raisins for time trial performance, power output, or rate of perceived exertion. Plus the athletes rated the sensory acceptance (taste, flavor, enjoyment) of the raisins higher than sports beans!

Bananas have also been suggested as an energy source during exercise, though there aren't as many studies comparing them to traditional sports products. One study compared bananas to a sports drink using equal rates of carbohydrate intake (Nieman et al, 2012). On two different occasions, 14 trained cyclists completed a 75 kilometer time trial. In one of the time trials, they drank the sports drink while in the other they ate bananas. Both the bananas and sports drink resulted in similar metabolic responses and the same level of performance in the time trial.

So what choice should I use?
The choice between utilizing a sports drink, gel, sport bean, chew/block, or real food item throughout an event is completely up to you. You have to consider the pros and cons of each item and how it settles with you during training. Sports nutrition is quite individualized, so you should practice with the items you feel will best fuel you and sit well in your stomach – and then take notes on how those work. Ask yourself questions like: Did you have any gastrointestinal distress? Did you feel fatigued mid-way through the run? Was there a sloshing feeling? You can use our training

and fueling log in the appendix to take notes on this so that you can nail down the products and amounts that work best for you.

In the meantime, though, here are a few of the pros and cons for each type of product you might consider:

Sports Drinks

Pros
- Addresses both hydration, electrolytes, and carbohydrate intake all in one package
- Particularly useful for shorter events due to ease of maintaining both fluid and carbohydrate balance (events between one hour and two and a half hours)
- Easy to find at grocery stores and sporting goods stores, though specialty products may require a little more work (ordering online or from a multisport store)

Cons
- Bulkier; heavier to carry
- Can be difficult to get enough carbohydrate without overdoing hydration during longer events (especially events over four hours)
- Can be difficult to plan for if you don't like what is served on the course (a fuel belt won't carry enough to sustain you for longer events if you can't replenish at the aid stations)

Real Foods
Includes items like raisins, bananas, Swedish fish, jellybeans, jam/honey on bread, pretzels, etc.

Pros
- Cheap
- Easy to find anywhere; readily available
- Research supports effectiveness similar to engineered sports products

Cons

- May settle heavily in your stomach
- Compared to gels/blocks, they can an take up more room on the bike and some can be difficult to carry on the run
- Depending on the item, they may get squished in transit
- With some real food options, you will need to drink electrolyte-enhanced water or take an electrolyte tab, as you may not be getting as much sodium as is ideal. For example, raisins only provide about 4 mg sodium per 100 calories, which is not enough to meet recommendations.

Gels

Pros

- Easy to carry and very light – you can store a lot of energy in a small space
- Found at most sporting goods stores in a variety of flavors

Cons

- Can be difficult to "get down"
- Unless you don't mind carrying half opened gels (a pet peeve of mine because the sticky stuff gets everywhere), you have to take down your nutrition at less frequent intervals. This strategy can cause some fatigue and stomach upset in certain individuals, but in others it may be fine.

Sports bars

Pros:

- May be more satisfying to eat during longer events when you start to feel hungry

Cons:

- These vary a lot in nutritional breakdown – read the label.
- Often contain fat and protein which slow digestion, so they may settle heavily in stomach
- May be difficult to meet carbohydrate needs using just these, depending on the product

Blocks/Sport Beans

Pros:
- Many find the taste/texture more palatable than gels
- Easy to control carbohydrate intake at frequent intervals (for example, one block every 15 minutes)

Cons:
- Product composition varies a lot between manufacturers, particularly in terms of electrolyte content
- May be bulkier to carry
- Some do not like having to constantly chew these products while exercising

On the following page is a breakdown of commonly used sports nutrition products as well as some "real food" options that you may choose to use for training. For each product, I have listed the amount of carbohydrate and the amount of sodium per serving size. Please keep in mind that these are for the current formulation of the product, because as we all know, manufacturers may change formulations or adapt the product as trends develop or research emerges.

Sample Fuel Choices:

Product	Grams of Carbohydrate	Sodium
GU Watermelon Chomps	23 grams in 4 chomps	50 mg
Stinger Honey Waffle	21 grams in 1 waffle	55 mg
Sport Beans	25 grams in 1 package	80 mg
GU Rocktane Gel	19 to 22 grams in 1 gel	125 mg
Gatorade	14 grams in 8 ounces	110 mg
Ironman Perform Drink	17 grams in 8 ounces	190 mg
Heed	27 grams in 1 scoop	40 mg
Perpetuem	27 grams in 1 scoop	110 mg
Perpetuem Solids	20 grams in 3 tablets	81 mg
Hammer Gel	21 to 22 grams in 1 gel	25 mg
UCAN (Pom-Blu drink)	32 grams in 1 packet	240 mg
Powerade	14 grams in 8 ounces	100 mg
Fig Newtons	22 grams in 2 small ones	125 mg
Swedish Fish	36 grams in 19 small candies	30 mg
Classic Thin Style Salted Pretzels (ex: Rold's Gold)	23 grams in 9 to 12 pretzels	300 to 500 mg
Slice of white bread with 2 tbsp jam	41 grams	180 mg
Raisins	30 grams in ¼ cup (slightly more or less depending on how packed they are)	4 mg

Nutrition information may change based on current manufacturing practices. Please check labels to verify current nutrition information.

Note that some options are rather low in sodium, so you may need to adjust for this by using an electrolyte-enhanced drink if you use these options.

A word of warning about balancing hydration and fuel...
Keep in mind that if you are using gels, sports beans/blocks, or food products, you'll want to hydrate with water or electrolyte drinks while eating them. This helps dilute the concentration of carbohydrates so your body can better absorb them. If you consume a sports drink at the same time as one of these other carbohydrate food choices, the concentration of carbohydrate in your stomach can be high enough to cause an upset stomach.

With some lower sodium fuel options, you will need to use an electrolyte drink or tab rather than just plain water as a hydration source. This is different than a sports drink, which contains extra carbohydrates. You can find electrolyte drinks that don't contain any carbohydrates, or you can also search for electrolyte tabs that you can chew or put in your water. For examples, because raisins are low in sodium, you'd definitely want a beverage that contained sodium, an electrolyte chew, or a sodium tablet.

Some people prefer using a combination of carbohydrate products, which is fine – you just have to put thought into spreading out the time between products. Perhaps you like to take in a gel once an hour with which you drink water, but then every 30 minutes between the gels you drink some sports drink. This fits in our range of 30-60 grams per hour, and because you are spreading it out, you shouldn't end up with an upset stomach.

TL;DR Tips on Fueling During Exercise

- For events lasting over an hour, carbohydrate intake improves performance.
- For events between one hour and three hours, aim for 30-60 grams of carbohydrate per hour, starting around the 30-45 minute mark.

- For events longer than three hours, you may need up to 90 grams of carbohydrate per hour, starting around the 30-45 minute mark.
- Your choice for fuel – whether sports drink, gel, sports beans/blocks, or real food – should depend on palatability, ease of use, energy levels during training, and gastrointestinal comfort. All of them could work well for you, and all have their own pros/cons.
- If you choose real food items or certain sports products, you may need to add additional sodium to your plan through an electrolyte-enhanced beverage, chew, or pill.
- Practice your fueling plan during training!

Spotlight Section: Choosing the Right Endurance Product

Have you ever walked into a running or multisport store and looked at the abundance of products on the shelf? Gels, shot blocks, drinks, fizz tabs, bars…it can be overwhelming! If you're wondering what products are best, you're not alone – it's a common question among many endurance athletes.

Factor #1: Macronutrient breakdown
Macronutrient breakdown refers to the amount of carbohydrate, protein, and fat in the product. Quick, pop quiz – which of these is essential for us to take in during exercise?

I hope you answered carbohydrate! During exercise lasting over an hour or so, you'll need to take in carbohydrates to supply your muscles with energy. For exercise lasting one to three hours, the recommended range is 30-60 grams of carbohydrate per hour. For exercise lasting longer than three hours, some athletes may need up to 90 grams of carbohydrate per hour to support the prolonged activity.

When you look at a product, check to be sure that it is a good source of carbohydrate. Look at the label and check the number of grams of carbohydrate listed in the nutrition facts. Be sure that you could picture yourself taking in an amount of that product that reaches our goal rates listed above.

Many "sports bars" targeted towards strength training athletes contain high levels of protein and low levels of carbohydrate – we want to avoid these. In fact, too much fat or protein in a product can be detrimental for endurance athletes during exercise for several reasons:
a) It slows digestion, meaning that energy might not get to your muscles very quickly.

b) It can cause gastrointestinal upset.

c) You might not get enough carbohydrate to supply your muscles if you're eating a product with excessive fat/protein.

Factor #2: Type of carbohydrate

Your body can only absorb so much of any one type of sugar at a time. It's important that your fuel choices contain multiple types of carbohydrate in order to maximize absorption of those sugars, as well as reduce the chances of gastrointestinal upset. Most engineered sports products are formulated with multiple types of sugars. You might notice the labels say it has a "2:1 glucose: fructose ratio" or "multiple transportable carbohydrates."

You can also check the ingredient list to look for multiple types of sugars/carbohydrate. Look for words like glucose, dextrose, fructose, sucrose, maltodextrin, honey, etc. Here are a few notes that may help you navigate your way through some confusing terms:

- Dextrose and pure corn syrup are both 100 percent glucose (so both are the same type of sugar).
- Sucrose is another word for "table sugar" – comprised of 50 percent glucose and 50 percent fructose (so it has two different types of sugar in one ingredient).
- Honey is 30 percent glucose, 40 percent fructose, and 20 percent water.
- High fructose corn syrup is typically 45 percent glucose and 55 percent fructose (data on HFCS is controversial in terms of health - it's your personal choice whether or not to use it during exercise).
- Agave nectars contain between 70-90 percent fructose and 10-30 percent glucose (yes, agave contains more fructose than HFCS! Keep in mind using almost all fructose can contribute to gastrointestinal upset, so I'd recommend avoiding products with agave)

- Maltodextrin is a polysaccharide comprised of several repeating glucose molecules (one type of sugar). Because maltodextrin comes in a chain of sugar molecules, it does have a lower osmolality compared to other products that can help reduce GI upset in some people. It's also often used because it's less sweet, so you avoid that 'sickly sweet' flavor present in some products. Ideally, it should be combined with another type of sugar in order to promote maximum absorption and energy production. Some companies do combine it with another source, while others don't.

Contrary to popular belief, maltodextrin is actually broken down quickly and is easily absorbed – similar to the rate of pure glucose. It is not a "slowly released carbohydrate." And this is fine, because we actually don't want a slow release during exercise; we want quickly absorbed carbs that supply our body with energy immediately. Because the insulin response is blunted during endurance exercise, we are not worried about large insulin spikes causing a sharp drop in blood sugar levels. Instead, we should be focused on getting quick, easily digestible carbohydrates regularly throughout exercise to provide a continuous supply of energy to the muscles.

Lastly, an important note related to ingredients. Real food products are highly underutilized in sports nutrition! Regular foods like bananas, raisins, dried cranberries, candies (Swedish fish or jelly beans), or Fig Newtons are all carbohydrate-rich choices that naturally contain different types of sugars. Multiple research studies prove that raisins and bananas work equally well compared to sports nutrition products in terms of performance. In addition, regular foods are often cheaper and more readily available.

Factor # 3: Gastrointestinal comfort

One of the biggest concerns among endurance athletes is gastrointestinal comfort while fueling during exercise. You can combat gastrointestinal upset through experimenting with different types of products, and by practicing your fueling plan regularly before race day.

Experiment with different types of products to see what sits best in your stomach. Everyone's body is individualized, so there's no blanket recommendation here. But a few tips...

- Certain people feel more comfortable using liquid sports drinks, as it's easier to match up fluid, fuel, and electrolytes all in one product. This is practical for shorter endurance events, like those lasting for two hours. For long events, though, many athletes prefer using other sources of fuel so as not to have so much sloshing (particularly during long road races or the run portion at the end of a triathlon). In addition, it can be difficult in longer events to focus only on sports drinks, as you may not be able to meet your hourly carbohydrate needs without a potential risk of overdrinking.
- Don't create an overly concentrated sports drink (you know, like when you throw two scoops of drink powder into your water bottle rather than one). The concentration of a sports drink impacts how quickly it can be absorbed in the stomach. Making it too concentrated can slow absorption, increase the risk of the "sloshing" feeling, and increase the risk of stomach upset. Follow the directions on the bottle. The manufacturers have taken the concentration into account when they recommend the mixing instructions.
- Be careful combining a solid product (like a gel or shot blocks) with a carb-based sports drink at the same time. It could create a situation in which it is too concentrated (similar to what was described above). This is relatively individualized, but there are a few ways to get around this

issue if you've struggled with GI upset because of it. If you prefer eating a lot of solid products or gels during your workout, you could combine these with an electrolyte-only drink (in other words, you get your carbs from the product and not the drink). Or, have your solid product with some water and then switch back to your carb-and-electrolyte-containing sports drink afterward.

- I personally recommend avoiding products that contain sugar alcohols, as these can cause gastrointestinal upset in some people. Check your product or food labels for ingredients like xylitol, mannitol, or maltitol (all sugar alcohols have that –ol ending in their name). If you find yourself experiencing GI upset after using a product with these, those sugar alcohols may be to blame.

Also, remember this: Just like you have to train your muscles to run or ride or swim, you have to train your gut. This is why it's important to start experimenting with your fuel choices early on during training. If you never fueled with any product during training, but decide to use them on race day, odds are you might experience some stomach upset. Instead, try your fueling options during training and choose one that you've found settles well in your stomach over time.

Factor #4: Practicality
Keep in mind the practicality of whatever fuel you choose. If you're going to be doing a three and a half hour endurance event, it's probably unlikely that you'll be able to carry enough drink with you to support your energy needs (unless of course you are using what's available on the course and you've practiced with that during training – which is smart!). Along the same lines, gels are light and easy to carry but during a six hour event you may get tired of the super sweet flavor and the texture, so you may want to alternate with another choice. Think about how much of each product you would need to support the goal rate of 30-60 grams of

carbohydrate per hour, and see if it's practical to carry and consume that much during your anticipated training/event time.

Factor #5: Electrolyte content
You'll also need to consider the electrolyte content of the products you'll be using. The most important electrolyte to be concerned about in endurance exercise is sodium. Losing too much sodium during an event may put you at greater risk for issues like heat cramping (anecdotal, but may play a role) or early fatigue. It may also increase the risk of hyponatremia (fluid overload is the primary factor causing hyponatremia, but sodium may contribute to this as well).

As discussed earlier, the ACSM recommends consuming 500 to 700 mg of sodium per liter of fluid you drink during any exercise that lasts more than an hour. Most commercial sports drinks will replenish around this rate. Certain sports drink products (Ironman Perform, for example) have a higher amount of sodium. This could be valuable if you are a heavy salt sweater or if it's an unusually warm day outside.

Be sure to carefully check other sports nutrition products or real food products you are going to use to see how much sodium is in them. Some are quite low. If you use one of these products during a 2-3+ hour event, and you combine this with only water, you may risk falling short in replenishing your sodium needs. There are electrolyte tablets or powders that can be added to plain water to supplement your use of solid products with additional sodium if the product itself falls short, or you can add a sprinkling of salt to your product/drink.

Factor #6: Personal Preference
Of course, to use any product, you'll want to enjoy the taste and texture. Don't force yourself to down something that isn't appealing simply because you heard it was a good product. As an

example, I don't like gels – that texture just makes me want to gag! But shot blocks, raisins, and sports drinks work fine for me. There are enough products and foods out there that can be successfully used without having to eat one you don't like.

Pulling it all together
Evaluate each of these six factors - and then practice, practice, practice! Use your fuel choice during long runs or rides in training, and then ask yourself:
- Did you feel energized during your workout?
- Did you hit the wall or bonk at all?
- Did this cause any gastrointestinal upset?
- Did it taste good?
- Could you see yourself using it during your event?
- Could you carry enough on the course to support your needs?

With all these tips and steps, you can be sure to start narrowing down a fuel choice that's right for you!

What about protein during exercise?

The verdict is still not clear regarding the influence of protein intake during endurance exercise. The thought behind consuming protein along with your carbohydrates, fluid, and electrolytes during exercise is that the protein may help prevent muscle damage and/or enhance performance.

Some research has not shown any benefit to endurance performance when protein was combined with carbohydrate for exercise fuel compared to simply consuming carbohydrate alone (Richardson et al, 2012; Osterberg et al, 2008). A few studies, though, have shown a positive effect when protein is added to exercise fuel, with improvements in run time to fatigue in intermittent exercise or improved cycling time trial performance (Alghannam, 2011; Cathcart et al, 2011).

However, there are methodological differences in many studies that may influence our ability to use this information practically. For example, in the study on cycling performance, the carbohydrate-only drink contained just one type of sugar (rather than the multiple types that are recommended), while the carbohydrate + protein beverage utilized three different types of sugar. This certainly could have influenced the results. In other trials, the amount of calories in the carbohydrate-only drink was less than that of the combined carbohydrate-protein beverage.

A meta-analysis showed that carbohydrate-protein beverages showed a positive impact on time to exhaustion performance (average 9 percent improvement) compared to a lower calorie carbohydrate-only beverage. However, *equal calorie* carbohydrate-only beverages showed the same increase in performance (average 10 percent improvement). Thus, the difference in many studies that suggest an improvement when adding protein to fuel during exercise may simply come from the additional calories rather than from the protein itself (Stearns et al, 2010).

It appears that if enough carbohydrate is consumed during endurance exercise, there is not much evidence to support adding protein for significant performance benefits. Also, the additional protein could hinder performance because protein-rich products can cause gastrointestinal upset during exercise.

My advice? If you're currently using a combined carbohydrate and protein beverage/food that works for you with no stomach upset, then there doesn't seem to be any reason to stop using that. However, if you're new to endurance sports or if you have been doing well on a low- or no-protein product, I'd recommend sticking with that product. At this time, there doesn't seem to be sufficient evidence to recommend switching to the products with protein, particularly when they can cause gastrointestinal upset.

I would say the area where this is lacking research and where the potential benefit may exist for the addition of protein is in very long endurance training and events, like in preparation for and in tackling a half ironman or ironman. In these cases, it *may* be beneficial to consume small amounts of protein during exercise. In particular, if you struggle to get enough carbohydrate to meet the recommendations, some minimal protein intake may help delay your time to fatigue.

Protein also may have a benefit on net muscular protein balance and supporting muscular recovery after many hours of exercise (Koopman et al, 2004). In any exercise, a very small proportion of energy is derived from protein. Over many hours of exercise, even this small proportion could add up and become substantial. In addition, during long events, athletes often feel hungry, and a small amount of protein may contribute to satiety. You may choose to get that protein through real foods that are naturally carbohydrate-rich and contain a little protein, adding a small amount of a protein-rich snack to your regimen, or choosing a beverage that has a high proportion of carbohydrates with a small amount of protein.

That being said, many athletes have difficulty over long events with protein because it does lead to slower digestion and can cause gastrointestinal upset. Carefully evaluate any product during training. Plus, keep in mind that for a half ironman or ironman race, your training sessions will (likely) be shorter than the event itself. Because of this, several athletes I know have been fine using a carb/protein mix during training, yet find themselves struggling with stomach upset in the event due to a longer time frame. Now, this is anecdotal and of course could possibly have happened when consuming carbohydrate-only products as well. However, it seems to be more prevalent in the carb-protein mix.

Bottom line: Choose products carefully, and if you decide to try a product with protein, be sure to experiment first during training.

TL;DR Tips on Protein During Exercise

- The research does not suggest a performance benefit to consuming protein during exercise as long as a sufficient amount of carbohydrate is consumed during moderate duration endurance events.
- There is little research on longer (half ironman/ironman) endurance events and concurrent protein/carbohydrate intake, so a potential benefit *may or may not* exist in these scenarios.
- Protein intake during exercise may increase the risk of gastrointestinal upset.
- Let your body be your guide.

One more reason to fuel during exercise…your immune system!

Consuming carbohydrate during exercise is not only essential for maximizing performance, but it is extremely important for your immune system as well. Long periods of exercise put your body under physiologic (and psychological) stress! In fact, endurance athletes often have higher rates of upper respiratory infections compared to those who don't have such an intensive exercise regimen. There are several hormonal and metabolic activities going on in your body during and after a long exercise session that contribute to the reduced immunity and increased infection risk.

The relationship between exercise and upper respiratory infections is actually quite interesting, and most researchers believe that it forms what's called a "J curve." In this model, those who don't exercise at all have a higher rate of colds compared to those who exercise moderately. However, that benefit only occurs to a certain point. When your training volume increases over that point, you the start to increase your risk of upper respiratory infections again. The J curve hasn't been definitively proven via randomized control research, but most epidemiological data seems to support it.

A review of over 60 studies on endurance athletes and nutrition found that the "most effective approach to maintain immune function in athletes" is to consume carbohydrates at the recommended amounts during extended exercise (Gunzer et al, 2012).

A proper overall training diet, rich in carbohydrate as well as micronutrients like vitamins and minerals, is also essential to immunity. Researchers have found that when athletes exercise in a carbohydrate depleted state, they experience higher levels of stress hormones and reduced immune function. Now, what's a carbohydrate depleted state? It could be a few things:

- Maybe you haven't been eating right throughout all of your training. You may have cut the carbohydrates in an attempt to lose weight (which, by the way, is generally not a good strategy for athletes!) and your body has been "running on empty," so to speak.
- Perhaps you were focusing on proper carbohydrate intake during exercise but outside of exercise you haven't paid as much attention to your diet.
- Or it could be that you were laser focused on eating right when training started, but now that you're logging more hours in your workouts, you need more food to support that.

Each of these scenarios could lead to a carbohydrate depleted state that can increase your risk of colds and poor immune function, as well as compromise training. This is an especially important concept to remember for athletes who consider the "train low, compete high" strategy, as it could lead to an increased risk of upper respiratory tract infections.

Recovery Nutrition

Recovery Nutrition

Recovery nutrition refers to the process of utilizing foods/drinks to help your muscles heal and bounce back after your workouts/races. It is especially important to focus on recovery after a very long/intense workout, after a race (where you are likely pushing yourself to a higher degree than many training situations), and if you are doing two-a-day workouts.

The foods or drinks used to help you recover after a long/tough workout should provide both carbohydrate and protein. Carbohydrate provides your muscles with the glycogen to replenish what you used while exercising, while protein helps with muscle repair. If you don't take in optimal amounts of carbohydrate in your recovery snack/meal, that protein also helps you to maximize glycogen synthesis from the available carbohydrate that you do take in (up to a certain degree) (Spaccarotella & Andzel, 2011). In addition, the combination of protein along with carbohydrate during recovery may help you to maintain a healthy body composition. In one study, this combination approach led to a greater amount of muscle mass and lesser amount of fat mass after eight weeks of aerobic training compared to those using a carbohydrate-only approach. (Cramer et al, 2012).

How much carbohydrate and protein do I need for recovery?

After a long training session or race (one and a half to two hours or longer), or an intense shorter session (one hour or longer), I would recommend about 1 to 1.2 grams of carbohydrate per kilogram of body weight within the first hour after exercise – preferably the first 30 minutes (Spaccarotella et al, 2011, Beeleen et al, 2010). For example, a 68 kilogram (150 pound) athlete would aim to take in between 68 and 82 grams of carbohydrate within that first hour.

Along with that amount of carbohydrate, I recommend 15 to 25 grams of protein (IOC, 2010; Beeleen et al, 2010).

After your initial recovery meal, ideally you would continue replenishing with carbohydrates at the 1-1.2 g/kg rate hourly for several hours, or until you eat a big meal.

What's the optimal carbohydrate to protein ratio?

A 3:1 or 4:1 carbohydrate to protein ratio has been shown to be optimal for recovery (Williams et al, 2003; Ivy et al, 2002; Zawadski, 1992). Let's say you're aiming to get 70 grams of carbohydrate after a workout. Based on the 3:1 or 4:1 ratio, ideally you'd want to take in 18 to 24 grams of protein with that. This fits in our recommended range of about 15 to 25 grams of protein after a workout. However, I'd recommend that you don't get overly tied down in this ratio. Simply eat something you like that is rich in carbohydrates and also provides some protein. There is no need for special recovery drinks, unless you find them beneficial and easy to get down.

What types of carbohydrate should I eat/drink during recovery?

Theoretically, it would seem that high glycemic index food choices would be the best for recovery. High glycemic index foods cause the blood sugar to rise quickly and consequently cause insulin to spike in order to remove the sugar from the blood stream. While normally we want to avoid these large ups and downs, during the post exercise time frame that would actually be a good thing. The function of insulin is to move sugar from the blood into cells, including those cells in your muscles which just used up a lot of glycogen during the training session or race, and now need to be replenished.

By eating high glycemic index foods post exercise, some studies have shown this allows muscles to rapidly re-saturate with glycogen, improving subsequent endurance capacity (Wong et al, 2009). Yet in other studies, despite the logical theory behind this, there has been no difference between low glycemic and high glycemic recovery meals on subsequent performance (Brown et al, 2012; Moore et al, 2011). And in some research, the reverse has occurred - low glycemic index choices showed better subsequent performance compared to high glycemic index choices, possibly by increasing fat oxidation in the subsequent exercise (Stevenson et al, 2005).

Though the research is unclear, if you are an athlete participating in intensive two-a-day training sessions, are training on a consecutive night-morning schedule, or have another race in the upcoming days, then it *may* be beneficial to aim for high glycemic index recovery choices based on the logic behind this theory. It is in these situations where quickly replenishing carbohydrate stores is essential.

However, for many recreational athletes, it is not important to get caught up in the specific GI of the carbohydrate choice. Research shows that as long as you consume an adequate amount of carbohydrate within the 24 hours following intense training/races, your muscles should recover fine and there should be no difference in performance for subsequent endurance training/events (Moore et al, 2011).

You can easily meet your needs for recovery through real foods versus engineered sports products. Recovery beverages can be convenient, and you may choose to use them, which is fine. But keep in mind that those products often don't contain vitamins, minerals, and phytochemicals like many "real food" products. Above all, your recovery choices should reflect what works for you in terms of palatability, gastrointestinal comfort, and perceived energy levels during subsequent training sessions.

What's so special about chocolate milk?

You may have heard all the hype in the media about low fat chocolate milk as a recovery beverage, and for good reason. Chocolate milk is inexpensive, easy to drink, and provides the ideal 3:1 to 4:1 carbohydrate to protein ratio.

Chocolate milk has been shown in many studies to be an ideal recovery beverage when consumed at a rate between 1 to 1.5 grams of carbohydrate per kilogram within one hour of exercise (Pritchett et al, 2012). Studies have shown equal or better recovery and subsequent endurance performance when comparing chocolate milk to fluid replacement drinks and carbohydrate recovery beverages (Thomas et al, 2009; Lunn et al, 2012; Ferguson-Stegall et al, 2011; Pritchett et al, 2009).

Some athletes have looked at me like I'm crazy when I suggest chocolate milk. "Don't you know they add a lot of sugar to that?!, I've heard.

Yes, there is added sugar – but that's what gives it the ideal carbohydrate to protein ratio. The specific ratio depends on the brand and how much sugar is added for that chocolaty deliciousness. For example, 1 cup of Hannaford Brand Low Fat Chocolate Milk contains 28 grams of carbohydrate and 9 grams of protein, for a carb:protein ratio of approximately 3:1. Nesquik Reduced Fat Chocolate Milk contains 29 grams of carbohydrate and 8 grams of protein per cup, for a carb:protein ratio closer to 4:1 (3.6 to 1 to be exact).

However, if we compared this to unflavored skim milk, we find that the skim milk contains 13 grams of carbohydrate and 8 grams of protein, thus giving us a carb:protein ratio of less than 2:1. While the regular skim milk would certainly be a healthier choice for everyday nutrition, for recovery we need that additional boost of carbohydrate.

Going by our recommended rate of about 1 to 1.2 grams of carbohydrate per kilogram, a 68 kilogram (150 pound) athlete would aim to drink about 2.5 to 3 cups of chocolate milk in the hour after a long workout – not a super large amount to consume, and possibly easier than trying to get down other types of food depending on your preference. If you're going to drink chocolate milk as a recovery beverage, aim for the low fat or nonfat versions, as in that immediate post-exercise period you are most concerned about getting enough carbohydrate and protein, and you don't want to "crowd out" those with too much fat.

What are some other good recovery options that combine carbohydrate and protein?

- Breakfast cereal and milk (which interestingly has been shown to lead to similar rates of muscle glycogen and protein synthesis when used for recovery compared to a commercial sports drink - Kammer et al, 2009).
- Bagel with nut butter and jelly
- Peanut butter & banana sandwich
- Fruit smoothie made with fruit and yogurt/milk *or* made with fruit, juice & whey protein powder
- Turkey sandwich plus a piece of fruit
- Homemade trail mix using cereal, pretzels, raisins, & nuts
- Baked potato topped with salsa and cooked ground turkey or beans
- Frozen waffle topped with fruit & nuts
- Rice or pasta with chicken

Keep in mind the portion size for each of these will depend on the specific amount of carbohydrate/protein you need, which is dependent on your weight.

A word of warning about recovery meals and snacks…

Many new athletes get overly caught up in recovery nutrition and believe they need some type of shake or recovery meal after every workout. Many also confuse commercial protein shakes, often marketed towards strength athletes, as being appropriate for endurance recovery (they're not, since they lack the right amount of carbohydrate).

Many recreational athletes with a low training volume – like some training casually for a 10K or for their first sprint triathlon – do not need to be overly concerned about recovery meals. For example, let's say you are that athlete training for your first sprint distance race. Most weeks, you swim twice a week for 30 minutes, bike twice a week for an hour, and run twice a week for 30-45 minutes. These workouts are short enough that your everyday meals and snacks are going to provide the recovery nutrients you need. The exception would be if you did a workout and you weren't planning to eat anything for several hours afterward – then it would certainly be reasonable to add a snack in there for recovery.

For these light to moderate intensity workouts of a short duration, though, that recovery snack doesn't have to be in the carbohydrate and protein ranges described earlier. In fact, those amounts would likely cause you to eat more than you burned off in a short training session, potentially affecting your weight throughout training. In these cases, a small snack that contains carbohydrate and protein should replenish you and hold you over until your next meal. A cup of yogurt topped with fruit or 1 cup of chocolate milk would both be excellent options, for example.

TL;DR Tips on Recovery Nutrition

- After a long training session or race (one and a half to two hours or longer), or an intense shorter session (one hour or longer), eat a combination of carbohydrates and protein to support recovery.

- Aim for 1 to 1.2 g carbohydrate/kg, plus 15-25 grams of protein within the first hour.
- Continue replenishing carbohydrate at this rate hourly for a few hours or until a big meal is eaten.
- For shorter and less intense workouts, a large recovery meal isn't needed, but a small snack could be appropriate if it will be several hours until your next meal.

Hot Topics

Hot Topics

Hot Topics: Fat Loading

"Fat loading" is the idea of utilizing a high fat diet (either in everyday eating, recovery nutrition, or pre-exercise meals) to shift the balance of fuel used in exercise. The hope is that eating a higher fat diet would lead to more fat burned during exercise (compared to carbohydrate), which would extend the amount of time one could exercise comfortably before "hitting the wall" (since we have so many more calories stored as fat compared to carbohydrate).

There are not many studies out there on fat-loading, and few that show any performance benefits. One study did find that participants consuming a high fat recovery diet had greater time-to-exhaustion performance in a subsequent cycling session (Ichinose et al, 2012). However, it's important to note that a) the high fat diet also provided more calories, which could have been an independent factor affecting recovery compared to the control diet; b) the cycling was only done at 65 percent of VO2 peak, but many athletes on race day may be exercising at higher levels than this; and c) these participants did not appear to be well trained, which could exacerbate the effect found in this study.

In fact, in another study where trained cyclists consumed a high fat diet for six days before exercise, fat loading actually caused detrimental effects (Havemann et al, 2006). The cyclists completed two weeklong trials, one on a high fat and one on a high carbohydrate diet. In each of the two scenarios, they completed 100 kilometer time trials on days one and eight, along with one hour of cycling on days three, five, and seven. While the high fat diet led to greater fat oxidation, it did not improve 100 kilometer time trial performance at all compared to a standard high carbohydrate diet. In addition, it also *decreased* the athletes' 1 kilometer sprint power. You know when you get to the end of your race and you want to be able to push it? You'll want that sprint power.

Many other studies have also shown no performance benefit to fat loading (Burke et al, 2000; 2001; 2002) and longer fat loading protocols of up to eight weeks show decreased endurance adaptations and significantly worsened performance (Helge et al, 1996).

Fat-loading can also make exercise feel harder, due to reduced glycogen availability. Many athletes who try to practice "fat-loading" fall short on the recommended intake of carbohydrate and protein. This can lead to reduced glycogen stores in the muscles and potentially impaired performance, as well as reduced protein availability for muscle repair and recovery.

A smarter strategy is to follow the basic nutrition advice given in this book – a plan rich in quality carbohydrates, adequate protein, and moderate amounts of fat. Along the same lines, focus on following your training plan, as training itself helps increase the body's capacity for fat oxidation. Trained muscles have greater mitochondrial and capillary density, which allows them to oxidize more fat. The trained body also has hormonal adaptations, delivers more blood/oxygen to muscles, and produces less lactic acid leading to a "glycogen sparing" effect that helps prolong the amount of time before glycogen depletion and fatigue. Training also increases the ability of the muscles to store glycogen, because as we know, during endurance exercise, you are always using a mixture of both carbohydrate and fat for fuel.

TL;DR Tips on Fat Loading

- Fat loading has not been proven to improve performance, and may hurt your performance.

- Eat a healthy diet that contains the proper amount of quality carbohydrates, adequate protein, and moderate amounts of fat to support training.

Hot Topics: "Train Low, Compete High"

Basically, the "train low, compete high" theory refers to training with lower glycogen stores, which is done by reducing carbohydrate intake in the training diet, not eating a meal leading up to that workout, or not taking in fuel during long workouts, and then competing in races with proper glycogen stores and fueling procedures. There is no standardized number or proportion of training sessions utilized in the literature, nor is there an established guideline among coaches and athletes that utilize this theory.

Sifting through the available evidence, there is some support that in short term training scenarios (3 to 10 weeks), the "train low, compete high" theory may benefit performance. This strategy is beneficial only when a *portion* of the workouts are completed on low glycogen availability or low glycogen fueling. It appears the mechanism for improvement is through increased training adaptations and improved enzymatic activity in the muscles that help breakdown carbohydrate/fat for energy (Hawley et al, 2010).

This does **not** mean that you should cut carbohydrates and train on low glycogen stores for every workout and then go to your race carb-loaded and stocked with gels. In fact, if you do this you may increase your risk of injury, weaken your immune system, and feel exhausted during training. You'll also likely experience some serious gastrointestinal side effects during your race because your body is not used to exercising and processing fuel at the same time (remember, we have to train our gut just like we have to train our muscles). Instead, this strategy should be for short term use and is only meant to be used for a small portion of the workouts.

Where could this practically fit into your training plan? Well, perhaps every few weeks you go out and do a two hour run or ride without ingesting carbohydrate (you should still bring fluids with electrolytes, but you can find those types of beverages without carbohydrate). The remainder of your training and your races would be done with proper glycogen stores and fueling. This may help you achieve some of the benefits from the theory.

Be aware, though, that the "train low, compete high" strategy can make the exercise *feel* harder despite the fact that you're working out at the same intensity you usually do. Because of this, some athletes are forced to stop their workout early – which certainly isn't what we're looking for, and in these cases could lead to overall poor (rather than improved) performance. In addition, we don't know whether this strategy may affect factors like injury risk and form, even when used on a short term basis. Plus, as we know, pre-exercise and during-exercise carbohydrate intake affects our immune system, so this strategy could put you at greater risk for issues like upper respiratory infections (Chen et al, 2008).

The bottom line: this is not necessary for most recreational athletes to dabble in, and even competitive athletes may find that the detrimental effect on perceived exertion may not be worth it. However, short term programs utilizing this method have sometimes shown improved performance. Keep in mind that utilizing this strategy long term, or incorrect use in too many training sessions, can be detrimental.

TL;DR Tips on Train Low, Compete High

- *Occasional* training sessions with low glycogen stores, either through a reduced intake of carbohydrate before or during exercise, *may* improve performance.
- Only occasional sessions should be used over a short term time frame – more is not better, and can hurt performance.
- These sessions may reduce immunity and make workouts feel harder.

- Avoid this if you're a recreational athlete. Competitive athletes may want to dabble in carefully.

Hot Topics: "Metabolic Efficiency"

Metabolic efficiency is another emerging concept in sports nutrition, which unfortunately (at the moment) lacks much research. There is always a careful balance in the sports nutrition world of making recommendations based on established research, and suggesting new theories and strategies that could potentially be successful, and we just don't know if this is one that is beneficial yet. Though there are athletes that utilize the concepts successfully, their stories are certainly filled with a bit of personal bias – plus there are plenty of athletes that have not been successful with it. I look forward to when there is finally research on this topic to give us more insight!

Metabolic efficiency is basically the body's ability to use stored fat and carbohydrate at different intensities. The goal of this strategy is to increase the body's ability to utilize more fat for energy at an increased range of intensities. Proponents say this is done by working on proper timing and composition of meals and snacks to optimize blood sugar levels surrounding workouts, as well as often reducing the amount of carbohydrate consumed during exercise.

Everyday diet adjustments are an essential component of metabolic efficiency (making it different than a focus solely on glycemic index before long runs/races). Those who venture into metabolic efficiency typically encourage a more moderate approach to carbohydrate intake in the everyday diet compared to current recommendations. Meals and snacks usually have a source of lean protein, healthy fat, and lots of fruits/vegetables. As needed to support training, you would incorporate healthy carbohydrate rich items like quinoa, brown rice, or sweet potatoes. Proponents support a periodized approach to sports nutrition where different meal composition is recommended at different points in the training cycle. During exercise, if you've had a proper meal/snack in advance, some proponents of metabolic efficiency training claim that you can run/ride without any fuel for up to two to three hours.

There are some valuable takeaway lessons to metabolic efficiency – namely that even endurance athletes don't have a license to overindulge in refined carbohydrates, which I've mentioned previously in this book, and that you should be adjusting your carbohydrate/calorie intake according to training load (aka periodization). However, while the remainder of the ideas sound great in theory, unfortunately they may not work for everyone. Some individuals may be able to tolerate and excel utilizing a lower carbohydrate intake, but many may experience fatigue and workouts can feel tougher.

Hypothetically, the main benefit to improving metabolic efficiency would relate to the fact that your body stores ample amounts of fat, so increasing the ability to utilize it at a given intensity would be a way for us to rely less on carbohydrate. However, as we've seen from the research in some of the glycemic index and fat loading studies, just because we increase fat oxidation doesn't necessarily mean it will translate to increased performance or a better rate of perceived exertion.

In addition, some of the metabolic efficiency proponents recommend consuming low levels of carbohydrate during training, and sometimes this leads to low calories overall. This is detrimental to training and performance, hands down. A slight decrease in calories could be beneficial if it led to weight loss while maintaining lean muscle mass (preferably in the off season), but cutting too low, particularly during lots of training, will lead to compromised performance.

The potential benefit I see – if work on metabolic efficiency was done correctly – is somewhat less reliance on carbohydrate intake during exercise itself, leading to less worry about gastrointestinal upset. Again, though, this may not be applicable or feasible for every athlete, and the longer you exercise, the more you will need to consider the importance of adequate carbohydrate intake during exercise.

The other benefit is that an athlete shifting from a diet high in *refined* carbohydrates to one of a more moderate intake of healthier carbohydrate sources could ultimately have a better overall health profile, particularly from a heart health (cholesterol/triglyceride profile) and potentially a weight standpoint.

It's clear that we need to see more evidence for this particular approach before veering away from what we know works (meaning what's been proven in research). We know that providing athletes with the recommended ranges of carbohydrate, and providing carbohydrate during exercise lasting longer than one hour, leads to better performance compared to when this is not done. Athletes attempting to create more 'metabolically efficient' bodies will likely have trouble doing so without the help of an expert to guide their diets and training cycles, and may end up with poor performance.

All this being said, I'm not an expert in metabolic efficiency and would never claim to be. If you're interested in learning more about this concept, the leaders in the field are Bob Seebohar and Dina Griffin, both of whom are also sports dietitians. Bob Seebohar has published a book on this topic.

TL;DR Tips on Metabolic Efficiency

- The goal of metabolic efficiency is to shift your body to burn more fat and less carbohydrate during exercise.
- There is little research available on the topic of improving metabolic efficiency in athletes, but there is plenty of

research supporting the other nutrition guidelines suggested in this book.

- Some athletes/coaches/nutritionists have anecdotal support for metabolic efficiency.
- Trying to alter your diet to become more metabolically efficient on your own will likely result in decreased performance. See a dietitian who specializes in this if you decide to try it out.

Hot Topics: Caffeine - Performance Enhancer?

Caffeine has been well established over the last decade to be a potential performance enhancer. Though the jury is still out on the exact mechanism, it is believed that caffeine works in several ways related to endurance performance (Goldstein et al, 2010):

- Caffeine can bind to adenosine receptors in the brain. Adenosine can make you feel tired, sleepy, or drowsy when it binds to its receptors. However, when caffeine blocks some of those receptors by binding to them instead, you become more alert.
- There may be a mechanism related to improved skeletal muscle performance, either through enhancing strength and/or neuromuscular function.
- Studies have shown that caffeine intake resulted in improved fuel utilization, encouraging a greater reliance on fat oxidation compared to glycogen (carbohydrate) utilization.
- It may increase endorphin secretions, which have a mood-boosting effect and may reduce pain perception during long bouts of endurance exercise.

The amount of caffeine that can improve endurance performance is in the range of 3 to 6 mg per kilogram of body weight, consumed about one hour before exercise (Goldstein et al, 2010). Doses above this range do not provide additional benefit (and may contribute to detrimental effects).

If you are a competitive college athlete, keep in mind the National Collegiate Athletic Association places upper limits on the amount of caffeine you can consume (which is tested via urine). For most people, the NCAA limit corresponds to caffeine doses greater than the range of 3-6 mg/kg. However, in some individuals, medical conditions, medications, or differences in biochemistry can result in caffeine being metabolized at different rates.

The International Olympic Committee previously included an upper limit on caffeine until 2004, but now it is simply on the monitored list of substances to track potential trends in misuse. If enough athletes were abusing caffeine, it could potentially be moved back to the prohibited list (World Anti-Doping Association, 2012).

Getting back to the recommended range, let's say you are an 80 kg athlete (175 pounds). Based on the 3 to 6 mg/kg range, the dose for potential performance enhancement would be approximately 240 to 480 mg of caffeine. This is equivalent to a few cups of coffee. It's important to note that even though caffeine is a mild diuretic, the current research does *not* suggest that doses in the range above contribute to dehydration or negative effects on fluid balance during exercise.

Some studies suggest that anhydrous forms of caffeine (like a caffeine pill, gel, or chewable tablet) may provide greater benefit compared to the ingestion of caffeine through coffee, teas or other forms (Goldstein et al, 2012). However, the caffeine in these drink/food sources do still lead to positive outcomes, are often more easily accessible, and newer research is suggesting there is not as big of a difference in performance enhancement when compared to anhydrous forms as once thought.

Whether or not you decide to utilize caffeine before a race depends on your personal habits, tolerance/sensitivity (which can be influenced by genetics), and medical conditions. If you regularly consume large quantities of caffeine, you may not see an additional performance benefit when you drink your standard amount of coffee on race day. However, you will likely see a decline in performance if you randomly decide to give up that caffeine on race day. If you're a caffeine junkie and want to have optimal use of it for a race, consider weaning off of it for week or so leading up to the event. This will decrease your body's reliance on it. Note that during this process you may experience caffeine withdrawal symptoms which include headaches and irritability. Although this is not pleasant, the benefits can be worth it. After you have been "clean" off caffeine for at least three to four days, when you go to use it on race day your body will get those desired stimulant effects again just like you're a caffeine newbie.

Along the same lines, if you never drink caffeinated beverages, you may see a performance boost with caffeine at the very low end of the 3 to 6 mg/kg range, since your body isn't used to the effects of caffeine. However, you may also experience side effects such as feeling restless or jittery. Caffeine can also cause stomach upset in some individuals. If this happens to you, you're probably better off just skipping it.

No matter what your situation, I can't stress enough that it is wise to practice with caffeine in training situations if you are planning to use it on race day. The way your body reacts to a certain food or substance at home on the couch can be very different when you are using it before exercise. Experiment during training to find out if this is right for you!

TL;DR Tips on Caffeine

- Use of caffeine is a personal choice.
- Caffeine can improve endurance performance at a range of 3 to 6 mg per kilogram of body weight, consumed about one hour before exercise. More is not better.
- If you regularly drink caffeine, cutting it out several days before the race and then re-introducing it on race day can enhance the performance benefit.

211

- High doses of caffeine used among those not used to it may cause jitters, irritation, and stomach upset.
- Don't try caffeine for the first time on race day – experiment during training if you plan to use it.

Hot Topics: Beetroot Juice - Performance Enhancer?

There has been some media attention about the potential benefits of beetroot juice (or sometimes simply called beet juice) for endurance athletes due to its high concentration of dietary nitrates. This juice comes from the root of the beet plant (those deep reddish/purplish vegetables) and the theory is that its dietary nitrates may help improve blood and oxygen flow to the muscles.

Dietary nitrates have traditionally been associated with harmful health effects. They are present as preservatives in processed meats like sausage and bacon, and have been linked to serious health problems like increased cancer risk. However, there is an interesting paradox that dietary nitrates found in vegetables seem to have beneficial, rather than harmful, effects. It is unclear exactly why nitrates in certain sources cause harmful effects and in other sources cause beneficial effects, but it is possible that the nitrates act in combination with other components inside vegetables, which protect us from any negative effects and create a positive impact (Murphy et al, 2012).

Here is a summary, study by study, of the available research at the time of publishing. I've broken it into two sections: the studies that suggest a benefit and those that suggest no benefit.

Research suggesting potential benefits:

Vanhatalo et al (2010) - Drinking 0.5 liters of beetroot juice led to a reduction in the physical demands of steady state exercise by around 4 percent, and this continued with daily consumption over five and 15 days. However, this study used a low calorie juice as a comparison, which can be a limitation since we don't know if it was the additional calories or the nitrates in the beetroot juice that led to the benefit.

Lansley et al (2011 - A): A single consumption of beetroot juice two and a half hours prior to two cycling time trials was found to increase power output in both time trials, and increased the speed of a 4 kilometer time trial by 2.8 percent and a 16.1 kilometer time trial by 2.7 percent.

Lansley et al (2011 - B): Nine athletes completed two different blinded trials, which involved drinking either regular beetroot juice or beetroot juice in which dietary nitrates had been removed. They drank 0.5 L of beetroot juice for five days. The physical demands of walking, moderate-intensity running, and high-intensity running were all less with the nitrate beetroot trial (as measured by O_2 consumption during exercise). In addition, the athletes increased their time to exhaustion during severe-intensity running by 15 percent with the regular beet juice.

Cermak et al (2012 - B) Other authors have experimented with smaller amounts of beetroot juice. In one study, 12 cyclists drank 140 ml (a little more than a half cup) of regular or nitrate-depleted beetroot juice each day for six days. They then completed 60 minutes of submaximal cycling followed by a 10 kilometer time trial. Compared to the nitrate-depleted juice, the nitrate-rich beetroot juice resulted in lower submaximal oxygen consumption (aka decreased physical workload at a given speed), as well as a faster time trial and greater power output.

Murphy et al (2012) – This study looked at the intake of the actual beet itself, rather than the juice. Eleven fit athletes, both men and women, completed a 5 kilometer time trial on two separate occasions. The researchers compared performance after eating 200 grams of baked beets (about 3.5 baked beets) versus eating cranberry relish (equal in calories but not a source of dietary nitrates). Average running velocity tended to be faster after consuming the beet compared to the cranberry relish, with a statistically significant increase in speed during the last 1.1 miles of the 5K.

Research suggesting no benefit:

Wilkerson et al (2012): In a 50 mile cycling time trial, beetroot juice did not have a statistically significant effect on performance or time.

Cermak et al (2012 - A): Twenty cyclists completed two 1-hour time trials – one after drinking 140 ml (a little over a half cup) regular beetroot juice and another where the researchers had removed the nitrates from the beetroot juice. There was no difference in performance, power output, or heart rate between the nitrate rich beetroot juice versus the juice without nitrates.

Christensen et al (2013): Ten elite cyclists drank 0.5 L of beetroot juice over a six day consumption period, and in a second trial drank the same amount of blackcurrant juice (which has a negligible nitrate content). There was no difference in submaximal exercise ability (120 minutes), time trial performance (400 calorie time trial), or power output.

Putting it all together
The bulk of the research seems to suggest that beetroot juice or even the beets themselves may provide a slight edge for highly competitive athletes. While not all studies showed a benefit, those that did generally found an increase in time trial performance by about 2-4 percent. Note that these studies have mostly been on well trained athletes. When researchers have examined the impact of beetroot juice in untrained populations, they have not seen a benefit. In addition, the potential benefit may only extend to your specific training discipline. For example, when researchers looked at the impact of beetroot juice on cross country skiers who ran a 5 kilometer trial, there was no effect – perhaps because running wasn't their preferred modality (Peacock et al, 2012).

The optimal dose based on this research is a half-liter of beetroot juice or three to four cooked beets, equating to 300-500 mg of dietary nitrates (Bescos et al, 2012). Pickled beets and other commercially processed options have a lower nitrate concentration than if you cook fresh beets at your home (Bednar et al, 1991). There are some newer beet juice "shots" available which boast a more concentrated source of nitrates, making it easier to get the amount for potential benefit without having to drink a half liter or eat such a large amount of freshly cooked beets.

It seems that the nitrate levels in the blood peak two to three hours after you eat or drink the beets, and then the levels stay elevated for another six to nine hours. If you decide to experiment with the use of beetroot juice in your training plan, you may want to try drinking a half-liter (or using a concentrated "shot" version) about three hours prior to a long training session/race (Jones et al, 2012). However, don't experiment with this for the first time at your big race! Remember our golden rule – don't do anything new on race day.

It is quite important to stick with dietary sources of nitrates rather than searching for a pill/supplement. Nitrate salts and pills can cause potential side effects which may be dangerous, causing problems like a severe drop in blood pressure, which can make you pass out. Some drugs for cardiovascular conditions may also react with these pills. And, perhaps most importantly, people can mistakenly purchase nitrite salts (emphasis on the i), rather than nitrate salts, which can cause extremely dangerous side effects in even small amounts. While nitrate is nontoxic up to rather high levels, nitrite can cause harmful effects at even low levels (Lundberg et al, 2011).

If you are planning to experiment with beetroot juice, keep in mind that even high *dietary* nitrate consumption may affect your blood pressure too. If you struggle with low blood pressure or are on blood pressure medication, you should approach your doctor before adding beetroot juice to your regimen. Lastly, you should be aware that beetroot juice may result in some temporary teeth and urine discoloration.

TL;DR Tips on Beetroot Juice

- Beetroot juice, through its dietary nitrates, may improve performance.
- Research suggests a dose of a half-liter of beetroot juice, three to four cooked beets, or a concentrated "beetroot shot" (produced specifically for endurance sports) taken approximately three hours before exercise.
- Don't try beetroot juice for the first time on race day, but instead experiment during training if you plan to use it.

Hot Topics: Leucine – Performance Enhancer?

Leucine is a branched chain amino acid and is one of our essential amino acids (meaning our body can't make it, so we have to eat it in food). During endurance exercise, the oxidation of leucine increases, which has propelled researchers to investigate the impact of leucine consumption during and after exercise. So does it help endurance athletes? Let's find out…

The Research

Recovery & Subsequent Performance

In one study, researchers compared two recovery meals consumed after two and a half hours of cycling intervals. One of the recovery meals provided a higher amount of leucine/protein compared to the other meal (but both contained sufficient carbohydrate and were equal in calories). After a day and a half of rest, the cyclists repeated a sprint performance test. The researchers found that those who had the recovery meal with higher amounts of leucine/protein experienced a 2.5 percent increase in sprint power and a 13 percent decrease in perceived tiredness during the sprints (Thomson et al, 2011). While a similar study found that leucine intake post-exercise did not improve subsequent sprint performance or power, it did reduce muscle tissue damage (Nelson et al, 2012).

Another study found that among trained canoeists, six weeks of leucine supplementation led to increased upper body power and work, increased total rowing time to exhaustion, and a decreased rate of perceived exertion (Crowe et al, 2006).

During Exercise

Other researchers have examined the impact on leucine intake during exercise. For example, Pasiakos et al (2011) compared the effects of two essential amino acid drinks – one with a higher leucine concentration – on fit adults during cycling exercise. They found that muscle protein synthesis was greater after using the leucine-enhanced drink. However, not all research has shown these same results, and protein intake during exercise can cause gastrointestinal upset in some athletes. In addition, we know that proper recovery methods after exercise enhance muscle protein synthesis, so the research is unclear about whether leucine during exercise is beneficial if proper recovery methods are used afterward.

Recommendations

Leucine may help with recovery and muscle protein synthesis after an endurance exercise session. It is possible that it may also help with subsequent performance. However, it does not appear that leucine intake *during* exercise helps to improve performance based on the current research.

There is no reason to spend money on pricey supplements, as selecting the correct food choices can provide all the leucine (and other amino acids) you need! For example, in the canoeist study, the athletes were supplemented with 45 milligrams of leucine per kilogram of body weight. For a 68 kilogram (150 pound) athlete, that's about 3060 milligrams, or 3 grams. And remember, this was per day, not just in the recovery meals.

If you take a look at our chart on the next page, you'll see it's easy to get that much each day by making choices consistent with recommendations for an athlete's diet.

Food	Leucine (grams)
Cottage Cheese – 1 cup	2.5
Chicken breast – 3 ounces	1.9
Steak (flank, braised) – 3 ounces	1.8
Turkey (light meat, roasted) – 3 ounces	1.8
Tuna (canned in water) – 3 ounces	1.6
Plain lowfat yogurt – 1 cup	1.3
Edamame – 1 cup	1.2
Skim Milk – 1 cup	0.8
Cheddar cheese – 1 ounce	0.7
Black beans – ½ cup	0.6
Peanut butter – 2 tbsp	0.5
Egg – 1 large	0.5
Almonds – 1 ounce	0.4

Source: USDA Nutrient Database

Knowing that leucine may be beneficial for recovery and subsequent exercise, you may wonder how this fits in with current recommendations for recovery meals/snacks. Choosing foods with leucine actually fits in perfectly with current recommendations. As a reminder, here are my recovery guidelines:

After a training session greater than an hour and a half (or a shorter but intense training session), especially if you are going to be exercising or competing again in a short time frame, it's important to pay attention to your recovery nutrition. Ideally, you'd aim for 1 to 1.2 grams of carbohydrate per kilogram of body weight every hour for several hours, or until you eat a large meal. These carbohydrates help to replenish the energy stores in your muscles.

Along with this, you'd aim for 15-25 grams of protein. In this 15-25 grams of protein, you can select quality sources that contain adequate amounts of leucine. In addition, you want to be sure you're getting a good source of protein during your meals throughout the rest of the day.

If you are doing shorter workouts, or if you are doing longer workouts but are not exercising again for a day or two, your everyday diet will likely help replenish your glycogen stores, ensure adequate leucine intake, and support muscular recovery. However, if you're not planning to eat a meal for several hours after your workout, I'd recommend a snack that provides both carbohydrate and protein.

If you find using protein powders is helpful and convenient in your recovery meals, a whey protein powder will provide a good amount of leucine. However, keep in mind that there may be quality control issues with many protein powders and that these powders are often more expensive compared to regular foods.

TL;DR Tips for Leucine:

- Leucine can be beneficial for improving muscular recovery after exercise, and may play a role in subsequent exercise performance.
- The research does not currently support a role for improved performance when using leucine during exercise.
- Leucine can be found in a wide variety of foods and does not have to be taken in supplement form.

Hot Topics: Nutrition for Injuries

Uh, oh. Whether you hit the pavement and heard a snap, or you hopped on the bike and that hip or knee pain just got worse, an injury is something that no athlete wants to deal with. While your doctor or physical therapist will take care of the medical and physiological side of recovery, there are a few nutrition tips that can help with proper recovery as well.

First, it is essential to get enough calories each day to support recovery in any serious injury, from a stress fracture to a torn ligament to a muscle strain. However, you also must be careful not to overeat. Even though an injury typically increases metabolic energy needs to support the healing process, you also are likely exercising much less due to that injury. This means you probably will not be able to eat the same diet you were eating during the bulk of training since your physical activity level is lower. Try to balance eating enough to support the recovery process but not eating so much that you start to gain weight.

During the recovery process, it is also important to get enough protein, as it is involved in muscle recovery, repair, and strengthening. If you have a ligament or tendon injury, you should know that protein has not been shown in research to help with collagen synthesis. However, with these injuries you often may engage in physical therapy to strengthen the muscles around those areas for recovery or after surgery. Because of this, it is important to get adequate protein intake with these injuries as well.

Keep in mind that adequate does not mean excessive, though. Excessive consumption of any macronutrient (carbohydrates, fat, or protein) can lead to weight gain if it pushes your calorie intake over the edge. While research is unclear on the exact amount to support healing, a protein intake of about 1.2 grams/kilogram of body weight has been suggested by several researchers (Tipton et al,

2010). This amount is normally part of an athlete's diet and can easily be met by including appropriate portions of high quality proteins at meals and snacks.

When you are training with an injury – perhaps in physical therapy, lightly with cross-training, or as you start to resume your regular routine – remember to fuel your muscles with carbohydrate during exercise lasting over an hour. As mentioned earlier in this book, athletes who don't take in carbohydrate during long exercise sessions end up stressing and suppressing their immune system. This is certainly not something you want going on during the healing process!

Interestingly, there are some nutrients that appear to be uniquely important to the healing process after an exercise-related injury. Here are a few tips highlighting some of the research:

- Omega 3 fatty acids, found in foods like fish, walnuts, and flax seed, are thought to be anti-inflammatory and may help with the recovery process.
- Vitamins C and E have been shown in research to reduce inflammatory markers following surgery for ACL injuries (Barker et al, 2009).
- Calcium and Vitamin D intake are particularly important for stress fractures, as they are involved in bone health.
- Zinc and Vitamin A are also micronutrients involved in immune responses (Tipton et al, 2010).
- One study found that current vitamin and dietary status, reflecting long term habits, may be an important contributor to post injury recovery (Barker et al, 2009). Translation: a balanced diet each day now could help you bounce back from an injury later!
- Alcohol, on the other hand, has been thought to impair muscle protein synthesis and may contribute to increased muscle loss (especially during an injury, which requires

immobilization for a period of time) (Tipton et al, 2010). It's wise to avoid excessive intake during an injury.

- Glucosamine sulfate, a component of healthy cartilage, which is sold in supplements, can help to reduce pain associated with knee osteoarthritis. It may also have a role in improving flexibility of certain areas after an injury, although the research on this is more controversial (Mayo Clinic, 2012).

TL;DR Tips on Nutrition for Injuries

- Eating a balanced diet with enough calories (but keeping in mind lower training volume) and adequate protein can help support injury recovery.
- Foods rich in omega-3s, calcium, Vitamin D, zinc, and Vitamin A may help improve recovery for certain injuries.

Hot Topics: Paleo – Is it for athletes?

The grapefruit diet, the Atkins diet, the cabbage soup diet – you've heard them all. But recently, a new diet has entered the scene – the Paleo diet. Also called the Stone Age diet or the Caveman diet, this meal plan suggests eating a diet closer to what the promoters feel our cavemen ancestors ate. It focuses on lean meat, fish, vegetables, and nuts, while completely cutting out dairy, grains, legumes, beans, processed oils, and sugar. Some versions also limit the fruit consumption to certain portions or times per day.

The diet is based on the theory that our core genetic makeup hasn't changed since the Paleolithic era, and in that era people didn't experience as much chronic disease. And so comes the conclusion that the diet cavemen ate is best for preventing chronic disease.

There are a few issues with this theory, though. Let's take a look…

1) The first major issue is that we don't know exactly how our ancestors ate, so the diet is based on our assumptions. While we can find out certain indications of what was eaten based on carbon dating, carved images, etc., no one can definitively tell us what our ancestors ate on a regular basis. In all reality, their diet probably wasn't quite as straight forward as the Paleo diet seems to indicate. Our ancestors likely moved around and ate whatever was available in the area they were living in or moving through.

In fact, newer research suggests that remnants of grain products have been found on the teeth of our Paleolithic ancestors. Now, does this mean they ate tons of grains? No, probably not. However, it's not as if we know exactly what they did or did not eat and in what amounts.

Some proponents of the Paleo diet will also claim that the body doesn't even need as much food, because our ancestors fasted many times when food wasn't available. The counterargument is this: don't you think if they had food readily available, they would have eaten it? It isn't likely that they voluntarily chose to fast.

2) This diet also assumes that the human body has not adapted to be able to eat grains and dairy, and that these foods contribute to overweight/obesity, heart disease, and other health problems. However, is there really solid evidence of this? Are we writing off the last 10,000 years of agriculture as something that none of us can really tolerate? It seems a bit hard to believe. Rates of obesity have skyrocketed in the last 30 years, not 10,000. Certainly there are individuals with lactose intolerance, celiac disease, or gluten sensitivities that may have to alter intake of these food groups. But I see no definitive scientific evidence that our bodies have not "adapted" to process grains and dairy. On the contrary, it seems that many generations before us led perfectly healthy lives eating these foods without struggling with epidemic proportions of obesity and cardiovascular disease.

3) The average life expectancy of a caveman was about 20 years. Now, this is of course skewed by the fact that there were lots of problems we consider minor now that did not have medical treatment back then – an infection or a broken ankle, for example. In those times, these issues could lead to death. But given that much of the population did not live older than this, it's hard to judge if the type of diet they ate truly prevented chronic disease, simply because most did not live long enough to develop chronic disease.

4) Quick, pretend you're a caveman and you want to get some food. What do you have to do? Go out and kill it. You want to go visit a new area? Guess you'll have to walk several miles over there. The activity level for this generation was likely much higher than our current activity level. It's a factor that we can't tease out of the equation.

All these assumptions and questions make this dietitian a bit skeptical.

Am I saying that there are no benefits to the Paleo diet? No, of course not. There certainly are some excellent parts of the diet – increased intake of vegetables and cutting out overly processed foods, for example. But there are some detrimental parts as well – namely a lack of certain micronutrients (like calcium), potentially too much saturated fat, and the fact that it's fairly restricting and many people may find that does not work for their lifestyle.

The reason many people lose weight and see improvements in their health on this diet comes from simply making healthier food choices. Individuals are cutting out refined, processed foods and choosing more produce and natural options. These changes can reduce the number of calories consumed to help aid in weight loss. Because you're eating more natural foods, there's less added fat and added sugar that contributes to other problems, like heart disease.

Is there research supporting any benefit to this diet? There are a few studies. For example, a 2006 study found that a Paleo diet improved glycemic control, BMI/weight, and cardiovascular risk factors compared to a diabetic diet among those with Type 2 diabetes (Jonsson et al, 2009).

There are several limitations to the conclusions that can be drawn, though. The study was small; there were only 13 participants. It was not blinded after initial diet selection. In addition, reading further into the study showed that the Paleo diet was lower in total calories and carbohydrates and higher in fruits and vegetables compared to the diabetes diet (average of 1581 ± 295 in the Paleo diet compared to 1878 ± 379 in the Diabetes diet). Could some of the proposed benefits, particularly weight, come from the fact that there were significantly less calories eaten on the Paleo diet, as opposed to the composition of the diet itself? I'd be inclined to say so.

Now, that study, as well as a few others, have looked at the Paleo diet with regards to populations with chronic diseases and obesity. And yes, in many studies, there were heart health or weight benefits. Whether that's from a paleo lifestyle itself – or, as I mentioned earlier, simply moving from tons of refined processed foods to more natural products – is yet to really be concluded. These same benefits are also seen with less restrictive meal plans, such as a vegetarian diet, a Mediterranean style diet, or the DASH diet.

Also, I think it's important to bring up another point. You are a bit different from many of the study populations, since you are an endurance athlete. So the question now becomes – what about athletes?

At the time of print, there is not one scientific study that has looked at the impact of the Paleo diet on athletes. However, there are plenty of studies supporting performance benefits to using the standard sports nutrition recommendations of healthy carbohydrates, adequate protein, and moderate fat.

So my view on this comes down to the following question: why adhere to such a strict diet when large bodies of research are lacking, and when there *is* research to support the benefits of much more flexible meal plans for athletes or simply balanced meal plans that reduce processed foods? There is no scientific reason to date that someone must cut out grains, beans, and dairy products from their diet if they currently tolerate them well. If a person has Celiac Disease or lactose intolerance, that's of course different. But for the majority, whole grains provide a healthy source of carbohydrates for energy, as well as heart-healthy and digestive-friendly fiber. Dairy products provide a major source of calcium in the Western diet, and while there are certainly additional sources of calcium outside of dairy products, if you like dairy and tolerate it, there's no reason to eliminate it from your diet. Along the same lines, beans and other legumes are great inexpensive sources of protein and fiber.

There are also the issues of lack of variety and cost associated with the Paleo diet. With meat being one of the most expensive items in our grocery cart, eating this way can be quite pricey. And after a while of following this diet strictly, you might find yourself craving more variety. The strict nature of this diet makes it much more likely for people to give up and rebound to old habits. And of course, there's the issue of global sustainability – it'd be impossible to support a global food supply on a Paleo type diet.

Lastly, even if you aimed to follow a strict Paleo diet, it'd be difficult to eat the foods in the manner they existed millions of years ago. Most of the meat available today is domesticated. Fruits and vegetables are grown on farms, not picked from the wild. There isn't much wild game running around that we're planning to eat. Not to mention, as soon as we start taking components of one diet and figuring out ways to tweak our favorite foods, we start adding back unhealthy components. I saw a "Paleo-friendly" chocolate cake recipe recently made with almond flour and coconut oil. Here's the thing – regardless of the fact that it doesn't have butter or real flour, chocolate cake is still chocolate cake, and I'm pretty sure cavemen weren't whipping these up for themselves.

The bottom line: The Paleo diet certainly has some advantageous components, like focusing on natural, unprocessed choices and increasing produce consumption. But for most people, there's no scientific reason to cut out broad categories of foods like whole grains, legumes, and dairy. And particularly for athletes, you'll likely need more carbohydrate than the standard Paelo proponents recommend. If you are considering Paleo to lose weight as an athlete, you can do the same by eating a balanced diet with a small caloric deficit. Certainly implement beneficial parts of the Paleo diet – less processed food and more produce – but there's no need to follow such a restrictive regimen.

If you already enjoy a Paleo lifestyle and you feel good on the diet, then by all means, do what feels right for you. But I'd encourage you to make sure you're meeting all your vitamin and mineral needs, and as an athlete, make sure you're incorporating Paleo-friendly sources of carbohydrate, particularly surrounding long training days.

TL;DR Tips on Paleo for Athletes

- Research does not currently support the use of a strict paleo-style diet for improved athletic performance.
- There is no health reason to remove grains, legumes, and dairy from the diet unless you have a medical indication to do so (like a gluten sensitivity or lactose intolerance).
- Certain concepts from the Paleo diet, like less processed foods and more produce, are valuable to implement in your diet.
- Because the Paleo diet is low in overall carbohydrate intake, you may experience fatigue and decreased endurance performance.
- If you decide to eat a Paleo style diet, be sure to add enough carbohydrates from starchy vegetables and fruits to support your training.

Hot Topics: Coconut water - "Natural sports drink?"

Coconut water is the new trend in beverages, with companies touting it as the best natural, rehydrating, anti-aging, good-for-athletes beverage out there. Different companies have made various claims, including promoting blanket statements like:
- It has more potassium than a banana, thus preventing cramping.
- It has natural energy for your endurance performance.
- It's been used throughout history for the prevention and treatment of dehydration.
- Athletes can use coconut water during exercise because it has sugar, salt, and other components needed in a sports beverage.

Are these true? Let's take a look…

What is coconut water?
Coconut water is different than coconut milk. Coconut water comes from the liquid found inside a coconut, while coconut milk comes from grinding up coconut meat and pressing out the liquid. Coconut milk is much higher in calories and fat, and is often used in cooking or baking.

For everyday (non-exercise) hydration:
One cup of coconut water provides about 50 calories and 10 grams of sugar (depending on the brand), so it's definitely a better option than sodas and fruit drinks (fruit drinks = not 100 percent juice) for every day hydration. If you hate drinking plain water and don't like seltzer either, coconut water could be something worth trying.

It's also got a whopping 400 to 500 mg of potassium per cup, which is essential for healthy hearts and muscles. Getting enough potassium each day and reducing your sodium intake, along with an overall healthy diet, can help lower your blood pressure too. That being said, potassium is found in fruits and vegetables which provide other nutritional benefits like fiber and phytochemicals. Coconut water is also a bit expensive, running about $2 or $3 per carton or bottle – versus $2 or $3 for a whole bunch of bananas.

What about use during exercise?
Generally, I don't recommend using coconut water as a replacement for sports drinks during tough workouts *unless* you are proactive about looking at the labels and potentially making a few adjustments. Most brands of coconut water provide less sodium than ideal, and some fall short on carbohydrates.

Most commercial brands range from 11 to 19 grams of carbohydrate per cup. Depending on your sweat test results and level of thirst, you may or may not be getting enough carbohydrate from this alone in workouts over an hour. For example, let's say you figured out that you need to drink about 4 ounces every 15 minutes for optimal hydration on a two and a half hour run (16 ounces per hour = 2 cups per hour = about 0.5L per hour). At this rate, you'd be taking in 22 to 38 grams of carbohydrate, depending on the brand of coconut water. Thus, brands containing carbohydrate in the higher end of the 11 to 19 grams/cup range could support your needs, but brands in the lower end of that range wouldn't reach the ideal 30 to 60 grams of carbohydrate per hour that you should be consuming. In this case, you may need an additional source of carbohydrate (perhaps a commercial sports product or a food like raisins).

In addition, most coconut water brands do not contain enough sodium for workouts longer than an hour. The ACSM recommendation is to take in 500 to 700 mg of sodium per liter of fluid that you drink. Most commercial brands of coconut water only provide approximately 110 to 185 mg per liter. Plus, some independent consumer lab tests have shown that some brands contained even less sodium than the labels claimed (Consumer Labs, 2011). If you decide to consume coconut water during a workout, you'll likely need to add a little salt to it or eat a salty food with it.

TL;DR Tips on Coconut Water

- Coconut water can be a choice for everyday hydration, but it does still contain calories and (natural) sugar. Be cautious sipping throughout the day if you are watching your weight, as liquid calories can add up quickly.
- Some brands of coconut water may not contain enough carbohydrate to support your fueling needs during exercise.
- Most brands of coconut water don't contain enough sodium to be used during exercise, but you can add salt or eat a salty food with the coconut water if you enjoy using it during workouts.

Hot topics: Organic vs. Conventional

Do you buy organic? Some people do and some people don't, but many are confused about what organic produce actually is and how it can affect our health. The word organic does not have to do with nutrition, but rather the way food is grown and processed. Farmers growing organic produce don't use chemical fertilizers or pesticides, and animals for meats and milk are raised without antibiotics or growth hormones.

Is there a difference in nutritional value?

A 2012 meta-analysis looked at 17 studies in humans and 223 studies of nutrient and contaminant levels in foods to examine the differences in nutritional content and pesticide content between organic and conventional foods (Smith-Spangler et al, 2012).

The findings? Nutritional content was basically identical between organic produce and conventional produce. Though this may be old news to some of you, there are a considerable number of people out there that falsely believe an organic apple will give them more nutrition than a conventional apple - so this research is important.

Of course, this study may overlook specific food differences in nutritional content. For example, a 2010 study found that organic strawberries were higher in Vitamin C compared to conventional strawberries – but they were also lower in potassium. While it's possible that certain produce items may have slight nutritional differences when grown organically, it seems that on a whole across your diet it's probably not clinically significant to your body.

Is there a difference in pesticide content?

What *did* differ between conventional and organic items was the pesticide content. This makes sense, as the purpose of organic farming is to avoid the use of potentially harmful pesticides. Over 35 percent of the conventionally grown produce contained pesticide residues, compared to just 7 percent of those organically grown.

This being said, few items exceeded the EPA-determined recommended limits for pesticide contamination, whether they were conventional or organic.

Even though there were few items that exceeded EPA pesticide limits, some individuals feel these limits are set too high (particularly for certain groups like children or pregnant women). Too many pesticides in the diet could potentially contribute to several health problems, though the research on this is somewhat controversial. If you are concerned about pesticides, the results of the 2012 study show that you can reduce your consumption of these pesticides by switching to organic produce.

Should I buy organic?

Your decision to purchase organic is a choice based on your own personal and financial values, of course. The one overarching message I'd like to get across is not to avoid eating produce simply because you're worried about pesticide residues. The benefits of eating a variety of conventional produce will likely outweigh the potential dangers of pesticide residues. Take care to wash your items well, and you can also choose to peel certain items (however, removing the peel also reduces the fiber/phytochemical content).

If you are worried about the pesticide content in produce, consider purchasing organic foods that are in the "Dirty Dozen" – a list from the Environmental Working Group of those produce items that tend to have the highest pesticide residues. You can probably feel comfortable purchasing conventional for their "Clean Fifteen" list, the produce that typically has the lowest pesticide content.

"Dirty Dozen" – Produce with highest pesticide residues	"Clean 15" – Produce with lowest pesticide residues
1. Apples	1 Onions
2. Celery	2. Corn
3. Bell peppers	3. Pineapples
4. Peaches	4. Avocado
5. Strawberries	5. Cabbage
6. Nectarines	6. Peas
7. Grapes	7. Asparagus
8. Spinach	8. Mangoes
9. Lettuce	9. Eggplant
10. Cucumbers	10. Kiwi
11. Blueberries	11. Cantaloupe
12. Potatoes	12. Sweet potatoes
	13. Grapefruit
	14. Watermelon
	15. Mushrooms

TL;DR Tips on Organics

- Organic and conventional produce are equal in nutritional value, but conventional produce contains more pesticide residues.
- The choice to use organic will be based on your personal values, beliefs, and finances.
- Certain produce items are more likely to have high pesticide residues compared to others.

Appendix:

Worksheets & Other Materials

Appendix: Worksheets and Other Materials

The following pages contain interactive worksheets that you may wish to use. These can help you develop an individualized nutrition plan to support your goals in distance running and the sport of triathlon.

The formatting of the worksheets and space for calculations in this book will not be as clear as printable full size pages. Knowing that many of you may wish to have these available to print and work through, by purchasing this book you receive free access to these printable worksheets through my website. To gain access, visit the link below and enter the password if asked for one.

Worksheet Link: http://www.inspiredwellnesssolutions.com/eat-to-peak-worksheets.html
Password (if asked for one): e2p2013

Assessing My Weight: Calculating My BMI

There are two different formulas for BMI below. One uses your weight in pounds while the other uses your weight in kilograms. Once you figure out your BMI, you can use the weight classification table to determine if you are in a healthy weight range. Keep in mind that BMI does not account for body composition. It is possible to fall into an "overweight" range yet still be healthy if you have a large proportion of muscle mass.

Pound formula:

$$\frac{\text{Weight in Pounds}}{\text{(height in inches x height in inches)}} \times 703 = \text{BMI}$$

Kilogram formula:

$$\frac{\text{Weight in Kilograms}}{\text{(height in meters x height in meters)}} = \text{BMI}$$

Example:
Jennifer weighs 168 pounds and is 5 foot 7 inches. Using the pound formula:

$$\frac{168 \text{ pounds}}{\text{(67 inches x 67 inches)}} \times 703 = 26$$

Weight Classification Table

BMI Range	Weight Classification
Under 18.5	Underweight
18.5-24.9	Normal Weight
25-29.9	Overweight
>30	Obese

My BMI and weight classification:

Use the space below to calculate your own BMI and assess your weight classification. Do you think this classification is accurate based on your body type and athletic abilities?

Calorie Estimator Worksheets

The formulas use your <u>weight in kilograms</u>. To determine this:

Weight in pounds _____ / 2.2 = _____ weight in kg

For some formulas, you may need your <u>height in centimeters</u>:

Height in inches _____ x 2.54 = _____height in cm

Method 1: Quick & Simple (easiest method but sometimes less accurate):
Step 1: Determine resting energy expenditure

Men: Weight in kilograms _____ x 24 = _____

Women: Weight in kilograms _____x 22 = _____

Step 2: Determine total calorie needs using activity factor (choose one activity factor that best matches your physical activity level and multiply your resting energy expenditure calculated above by that number)

X 1.2 for sedentary day/job and/or little physical activity = _____

X 1.3 for a few days of light activity = _____

X 1.5-1.6 for up to 1 hour of moderate to intense physical activity/day = _____

X 1.7 for 1-2 hours of moderate to intense physical activity/day = _____

X 1.9-2.1 for very active job (construction worker for example), full time athletes, and/or multiple hours of physical activity everyday = _____

Method 2: Mifflin equation (*best equation to use if you are overweight/obese*):

Step 1: Determine resting energy expenditure

Men: (10 x wt in kg) + (6.25 x ht in cm) – (5 x age) + 5 = _____

Women: (10 x wt in kg) + (6.25 x ht in cm) – (5 x age) – 161 =

_____

Step 2: Determine total calorie needs using activity factor (choose one activity factor that best matches your physical activity level and multiply your resting energy expenditure calculated above by that number)

X 1.2 for sedentary = _____

X 1.375 for light activity (1-3x/week) = _____

X 1.55 for moderate activity (3-5x/week or more days at an easier intensity) = _____

X 1.75 for heavy activity (6-7x/week) = _____

X 1.9 to 2.1 very heavy (exerting job; two-a-days; full time athletes) = _____

Calorie and Weight Analysis:

Based on these equations, my calorie needs are:
_____.

Am I trying to lose weight? ☐ Yes   ☐ No

If yes, weight loss can be accomplished by a small reduction in calories. You can subtract out between 10-20% of daily calories, or up to approximately 500 calories per day – whichever is *less*.

10% of my daily needs = (_____ my calorie needs) x (0.10) = _____ calories to cut

20% of my daily needs = (_____ my calorie needs) x (0.20) = _____ calories to cut

If these numbers are more than 500 calories, ignore them and cut a maximum of 250 to 500 per day. If the 20% estimate is less than 500 calories, do not cut more than that number of calories.

My Daily Macronutrient Needs Worksheet

My weight in kilograms:
_____ wt in pounds / 2.2 = _____ kg

1) Carbohydrate needs
Select the category that most closely fits your training plan. Choose one number from that range and multiply by your weight in kilograms to determine the amount of carbohydrate needed per day.

☐ 3-5 g/kg for very light training (<1 hour daily; 1 hour some days) = _____ grams

☐ 5-7 g/kg for light to moderate training – 1-1.5 hrs/day = _____ grams

☐ 6-10 g/kg for moderate to high intensity – 1 to 3 hrs/day = _____ grams

☐ 8-12 g/kg for very high intensity - >4 to 5 hrs/day = _____ grams

2) Protein needs
Select the category that most closely fits your training plan. Choose a number from that range and multiply by your weight in kilograms to determine the amount of protein needed per day.

☐ 0.8 to 1 g/kg for fitness exercising = _____ grams

☐ 1.2 to 1.7 g/kg for light to moderate training = _____ grams

☐ 1.4 to 2 g/kg for heavy training = _____ grams

3) Fat needs

Figure these out by taking your total estimated calorie needs (found in the last worksheet) and subtracting the calories from carbohydrate and protein.

_____ grams of carbohydrate x 4 = _____ calories from carbohydrate

_____ grams of protein x 4 = _____ calories from protein

_____ total calories I need each day – (_____ calories from carbohydrate) – (_____ calories from protein) = _____ remaining calories for fat

_____ remaining calories for fat / 9 = _____ grams of fat per day

4) Double check

Because you're estimating these on your own, sometimes you may accidentally choose a number or range that's not actually appropriate, and this can throw off your calculations. To double check your estimates, try figuring out the percentage of carbohydrates, protein, and fat that you're eating.

Notice each of the following calculations uses calories from each macronutrient (which you found in step 3 above), not grams.

_____ calories from carbohydrate / _____ total calories I need = _____% calories from carbohydrate

_____ calories from protein / _____ total calories I need = _____% calories from protein

_____ calories from fat / _____ total calories I need = _____% calories from fat

Appropriate ranges are approximately 50-65 percent carbohydrate, 20-30 percent fat, and 10-20 percent protein. If each number above falls in these ranges, you can be fairly confident that you have good estimates.

Pre-Exercise Meal Worksheet

My weight in kilograms:

_____ wt in pounds / 2.2 = _____ kg

Multiply your weight in kilograms by the number of hours prior to eating using the calculation below. You can experiment with different timing strategies during training to see which works best for you.

3-4 hours before*
____ kg x 3 = _____ g carbohydrate in meal
____ kg x 4 = _____ g carbohydrate in meal

2-3 hours before
____ kg x 2 = _____ g carbohydrate in meal
____ kg x 3 = _____ g carbohydrate in meal

1 hours before*
____ kg x 1 = _____ g carbohydrate in meal

*= Generally most successful options.

Meal tips:
- Include carbohydrate and some protein (eggs, nut butter, lean meat, dairy) with meals further out leaving flexibility for more protein, and meals closer to exercise calling for less protein
- Avoid too much fat or fiber
- Include adequate fluids

Hydration Needs – Sweat Test Worksheet

Follow each step below to determine your individualized sweat rate, which can help you plan appropriately for your hydration needs.

Before your workout:

1) Weigh yourself at the start of your workout = _____ pounds

2) Write down the amount of beverage you are taking with you (or that you will be setting aside for a fuel stop) before the start of your workout. You should set aside a certain amount for the purpose of this exercise.

Amount of beverage at start of workout = _____ ounces at start

After your workout:

3) Weigh yourself at the end of your workout = _____ pounds

4) Complete these calculations regarding your weight change:

[Start weight of _____] – [end weight of _____] = _____ pounds lost

Note – if you weigh more than you did at the start of your workout, you are likely over hydrating. If you lost more than 2-3% of your initial body weight, you are likely under hydrating.

_____ pounds lost x 16 = _____ounces (oz) weight lost during exercise [A]

5) Complete these calculations regarding your beverage intake:

You had a certain amount of beverage that you set aside at the start to take with you or set up at a fuel stop. How much of this was left over at the end that you did not drink?

Amount of beverage leftover at end of workout = _____ ounces

[_____ oz of beverage at start] – [_____ oz of beverage at finish] = _____ oz consumed [B]

6) Determine your sweat rate using these numbers:

_____ oz weight lost [A] + _____ oz fluid consumed [B] = ____ total oz of sweat lost [C]

_____ oz of sweat lost [C] / _____ hours of exercise = _____ oz of sweat per hour [D]

That last number is your hourly sweat rate. This is the amount of hydration that would maintain your body weight during exercise. You should not go over this amount, as that increases your risk of hyponatremia. You can aim to consume right around or slightly less than your sweat rate each hour in order to maintain hydration without risking hyponatremia.

Additional Notes
- Keep in mind that your sweat rate may vary based on the type of exercise – i.e. a bike ride versus a run. You may wish to conduct separate tests for each.
- Weather conditions affect sweat rate. You may want to conduct a sweat test under the conditions you expect on race day. Or, you may wish to try a few sweat tests on different days under different conditions so you know how your sweat rate varies between those conditions.

Hydration Needs – Sweat Test Worksheet – Sample Calculations

Below is an example of an athlete's sweat test calculations.

Before your workout:
1) Weigh yourself at the start of your workout = 170 pounds
2) Amount of beverage at start of workout = 32 ounces at start

After your workout:
3) Weigh yourself at the end of your workout = 166 pounds
4) Complete these calculations regarding your weight change:

[Start weight of 170] – [end weight of 166] = 4 pounds lost

4 pounds lost x 16 = 64 ounces (oz) weight lost during exercise **[A]**

5) Complete these calculations regarding your beverage intake:

Amount of beverage leftover at end of workout = 0 ounces

[32 oz of beverage at start] – [0 oz of beverage at finish] =
   32 oz consumed **[B]**

6) Determine your sweat rate using these numbers:
64 oz weight lost **[A]** + 32 oz fluid consumed **[B]** = 96 total oz of sweat lost **[C]**

96 oz of sweat lost **[C]** / 3 hours of exercise = 32 oz of sweat per hour **[D]**

This athlete's sweat rate was 32 ounces per hour. Under similar conditions, he might aim for approximately 30 ounces per hour to maintain hydration.

Daily Food Log

Date: _____   Day of the week: _____

Time of day	Meal, snack, or drink. Include the type of food, any preparation details (i.e. fried vs. baked), and quantity (1/2 cup of rice; 10 strawberries; etc).	-Notes about how you felt before eating (hungry, bored, tired...) -Notes about training (i.e. "before bike ride" or "during run"

Any important notes about the day? (For example, "this was the night I went out for Kim's birthday" or "this was the day before the half ironman").

_____

_____

Training and Fueling Log

Workout Description

☐ Run   ☐ Bike   ☐ Swim   ☐ Other: _____

Type of workout? (speed, tempo, long run/ride, etc.): _____

Mileage/Distance: _____   Time: _____

Pace: _____

Perceived difficulty of workout: _____
[You can use a scale of 1 to 10 – 1 being a very easy walk and 10 being an all-out sprint]

Hydration
Total ounces during session: _____   Ounces per hour: _____

Fueling (for sessions lasting >1 hour)
Fuel source (gel, sports drink, bananas, etc.): _____

Amount of fuel source during entire session: _____

Amount of total carbohydrate during entire session: _____

Approximate grams of carbohydrate/hour: _____

Any gastrointestinal issues:
_____

Compared to other fueling methods I've tried, this one was:
☐ Better   ☐ Worse   ☐ No difference

Any other notes about training session:
_____

Cheat Sheet for Exercise Fueling

Pre-Exercise Meal

Time frame before training/race	Guidelines
3-4 hours before	3 to 4 g carbohyrate/kg Moderate protein, avoid too much fat/fiber
2-3 hours before	2 to 3 g carbohyrate/kg Moderate protein, low in fats/fiber
1 hour before	1 g carbohyrate/kg Easy to digest, low in fat/fiber
"I hate eating before training/races."	Bigger dinner the night before; sports drink, gel, or carbohydrate-rich snack a few minutes before heading out

Hydration

General guidelines: For individualized recommendations, perform a sweat test. **Above all, let physiologic symptoms of thirst (dry mouth, craving water) or overdrinking (nausea, sloshing) guide hydration.**

2 to 4 hours before	5 to 10 ml/kg of water/sports drink – for most athletes, this would be approximately 10-25 ounces
10-15 minutes before	5 to 10 ounces water/sports drink, guided by thirst
Every 15 to 20 minutes of event	3-8 ounces fluid (estimate) *Preferably generalized plan using sweat test, then guide by thirst*
After event	Drink 16 to 24 ounces fluid for each pound lost.

Electrolytes - Sodium
- Sodium is important in events lasting over one hour
- 500 to 700 mg sodium per liter of fluid consumed during training, either through a beverage or food item
- May need to increase for heavy salt sweaters or hot weather conditions

Fueling with carbohydrates during exercise:

Time Frame	Amount of Carbohydrate
Less than 45 minutes	Not needed
45 minutes to 1:15	No physiologic need, but mouth rinse and small amounts of carbohydrate may be beneficial
1:15 to 3 hours	30 to 60 grams per hour
Longer 3 hours	Up to 90 grams per hour

Recovery Nutrition:
- 1-1.2 g/kg carbohydrate along with 15-25 grams of protein within first hour
- Repeat hourly for a few hours, or until a large meal is eaten

Triathlon Race Day Checklist:

Below you will find a handy checklist of items that you may need for your upcoming race. Note that many people will not need every item. You can pick and choose items to develop your own customized list. Keep it with your gear or transition bag so that you can double check what you have before heading off to the race!

☐ Swimsuit or tri-suit
☐ Goggles
☐ Anti-fog solution for goggles
☐ Spare pair of goggles (just in case yours break)!
☐ Wetsuit
☐ Body glide
☐ Towels (you may want one to dry off with after the swim and a smaller one to wipe your feet on at transition)
☐ Water bottle(s) – including a spare if you like to rinse feet at transition
☐ Clothes for cycling/running (if you're not in a tri-suit)
☐ Socks
☐ Race belt
☐ Race number (if you've already picked it up)
☐ Watch/heart rate monitor
☐ Bike (double check handle bars are plugged)
☐ Helmet
☐ Cycling shoes
☐ Pump
☐ Patch kit
☐ Spare tube
☐ CO_2 Cartridges
☐ Cycling gloves
☐ Sun glasses
☐ Running sneakers
☐ Hat/visor
☐ Fuel belt
☐ Fuel sources – gels, sports drink, etc.
☐ ID and USAT Card
☐ Sunscreen

References

Selected References

Academy of Nutrition and Dietetics (AND). (2013). Eat Right for Endurance. Retrieved from: http://www.eatright.org/Public/content.aspx?id=7085

Alberici JC, Farrell PA, Kris-Etherton PM, Shivley CA. Effects of preexercise candy bar ingestion on glycemic response, substrate utilization, and performance. Int J Sport Nutr Exerc Metab. 1993;3:323–333.

Alghannam AF. (2011). Carbohydrate-protein ingestion improves subsequent running capacity towards the end of a football-specific intermittent exercise. Appl Physiol Nutr Metab; 36(5):748-57.

American Cancer Society. (2008). Broccoli. Retrieved from: http://www.cancer.org/treatment/treatmentsandsideeffects/complementaryandalternativeme dicine/dietandnutrition/broccoli

American College of Sports Medicine (ACSM). (2007). Position stand: Exercise & Fluid Replacement. Medicine & Science in Sports & Exercise; 39(2): 377-390.

American Council on Exercise (ACE) Lifestyle & Weight Management Coach Manual. Body Fat Classifications. Online chart found at: http://www.acefitness.org/acefit/healthy_living_tools_content.aspx?id=2#sthash.yaylJ0uG.dp bs

American Institute for Cancer Research (AICR) (2011). Foods That Fight Cancer: Grapes and Grape Juice. Retrieved from: http://www.aicr.org/foods-that-fight-cancer/foodsthatfightcancer_grapes_and_grape_juice.html

American Optometric Association. (2012). Lutein & Zeaxanthin. Retrieved from http://www.aoa.org/x11815.xml

Anastasiou C, Kavouras S, Arnaoutis G, Gioxari A, Kollia M, Botoula B, Sidossis LS. (2009). Sodium Replacement and Plasma Sodium Drop During Exercise in the Heat When Fluid Intake Matches Fluid Loss. J Athl Train; 44(2): 117–123.

Angeline ME, Gee AO, Shindle M, Warren RF, Rodeo SA. (2013). The effects of vitamin D deficiency in athletes. Am J Sports Med; 41(2):461-4.

Ashraf R, Aamir K, Shaikh AR, Ahmed T. (2005). Effects of garlic on dyslipidemia in patients with type 2 diabetes mellitus. J Ayub Med Coll Abbottabad; 17(3):60-4.

Assunção ML, Ferreira HS, dos Santos AF, Cabral CR Jr, Florêncio TM. (2009). Effects of dietary coconut oil on the biochemical and anthropometric profiles of women presenting abdominal obesity. Lipids; 44(7):593-601.

Atkinson FS, Foster-Powell K, Brand-Miller JC. (2008). International tables of glycemic index and glycemic load values: 2008. Diabetes Care; 31(12):2281-3.

Baker L, Lang J, Kenney WL. (2008). Quantitative analysis of serum sodium concentration after prolonged running in the heat. J. Appl. Physiol; 105:1 91-99.

Barker T, Leonard SW, Hansen J, Trawick RH, Ingram R, Burdett G, Lebold KM, Walker JA, Traber MG. (2009). Vitamin E and C supplementation does not ameliorate muscle dysfunction after anterior cruciate ligament surgery. Free Radic Biol Med; 47(11):1611-8.

Barker T, Leonard SW, Trawick RH, Walker JA, Traber MG. (2009). Antioxidant supplementation lowers circulating IGF-1 but not F(2)-isoprostanes immediately following anterior cruciate ligament surgery. Redox Rep;14(5):221-6.

Barr SI. (1999). Effects of dehydration on exercise performance. Can J Appl Physiol; 24(2):164-72.

Bednar CM, Kies C, Carlson M. (1991). Nitrate-nitrite levels in commercially processed and home processed beets and spinach. Plant Foods Hum Nutr; 41(3):261-8.

Beelen M, Burke LM, Gibala MJ, van Loon L JC. (2010). Nutritional strategies to promote postexercise recovery. Int J Sport Nutr Exerc Metab; 20(6):515-32.

Bennett CB, Chilibeck PD, Barss T, Vatanparast H, Vandenberg A, Zello GA. (2012). Metabolism and performance during extended high-intensity intermittent exercise after consumption of low- and high-glycaemic index pre-exercise meals. Br J Nutr; 108 Suppl 1:S81-90.

Beis LY, Wright-Whyte M, Fudge B, Noakes T, Pitsiladis YP. (2012). Drinking behaviors of elite male runners during marathon competition. Clin J Sport Med; 22(3):254-61.

Bescós R, Ferrer-Roca V, Galilea PA, Roig A, Drobnic F, Sureda A, Martorell M, Cordova A, Tur JA, Pons A. (2012). Sodium nitrate supplementation does not enhance performance of endurance athletes. Med Sci Sports Exerc; 44(12):2400-9.

Brown LJ, Midgley AW, Vince RV, Madden LA, McNaughton LR. (2012). High versus low glycemic index 3-h recovery diets following glycogen-depleting exercise has no effect on subsequent 5-km cycling time trial performance. J Sci Med Sport; pii: S1440-2440(12)00208-3.

Buono M, Ball K, Kolkhorst F. (2007). Sodium ion concentration vs. sweat rate relationship in humans. J. Appl. Physiol.; 103:3 990-994.

Burke LM, Angus DJ, Cox GR, Cummins NK, Febbraio MA, Gawthorn K, Hawley JA, Minehan M, Martin DT, and Hargreaves M. (2000). Effect of fat adaptation and carbohydrate restoration on metabolism and performance during prolonged cycling. J Appl Physiol 89: 2413–2421.

Burke LM, Hawley JA, Angus DJ, Cox GR, Clark SA, Cummins NK, Desbrow B, and Hargreaves M. (2002). Adaptations to short-term high-fat diet persist during exercise despite high carbohydrate availability. Med Sci Sports Exerc 34: 83–91.

260

Burke LM, Hawley JA, Wong SH, Jeukendrup AE. (2011). Carbohydrates for training and competition. J Sports Sci; 29 Suppl 1:S17-27.

Buskirk, E., and W. Beetham. Dehydration and body temperature as a result of marathon running. Medicina Sportiva 14:493-506, 1960.

Campbell C, Prince D, Braun M, Applegate E, Casazza GA. Carbohydrate-supplement form and exercise performance. Int J Sport Nutr Exerc Metab. 2008;18(2):179–190.

Carey AL, Staudacher HM, Cummings NK, Stepto NK, Nikolopoulos V, Burke LM, and Hawley JA. (2001). Effects of fat adaptation and carbohydrate restoration on prolonged endurance exercise. J Appl Physiol 91: 115–122.

Cathcart AJ, Murgatroyd SR, McNab A, Whyte LJ, Easton C. (2011). Combined carbohydrate-protein supplementation improves competitive endurance exercise performance in the heat. Eur J Appl Physiol; 111(9):2051-61.

Cermak NM, Gibala MJ, van Loon LJ. (2012). Nitrate supplementation's improvement of 10-km time-trial performance in trained cyclists. Int J Sport Nutr Exerc Metab; 22(1):64-71.

Cermak NM, Res P, Stinkens R, Lundberg JO, Gibala MJ, van Loon L JC. No improvement in endurance performance after a single dose of beetroot juice. Int J Sport Nutr Exerc Metab. 2012 Dec;22(6):470-8.

Chanet A, Milenkovic D, Manach C, Mazur A, Morand C. (2012). Citrus flavanones: what is their role in cardiovascular protection? J Agric Food Chem; 60(36):8809-22.

Chen YJ, Wong SH, Chan CO, Wong CK, Lam CW, Siu PM. (2009). Effects of glycemic index meal and CHO-electrolyte drink on cytokine response and run performance in endurance athletes. J Sci Med Sport; 12(6):697-703.

Chen YJ, Wong SH, Wong CK, Lam CW, Huang YJ, Siu PM. (2008). Effect of preexercise meals with different glycemic indices and loads on metabolic responses and endurance running. Int J Sport Nutr Exerc Metab; 18(3):281-300.

Chen YJ, Wong SH, Wong CK, Lam CW, Huang YJ, Siu PM. (2008). The effect of a pre-exercise carbohydrate meal on immune responses to an endurance performance run. Retrieved from: Br J Nutr; 100(6):1260-8.

Chen Y, Wong SH, Xu X, Hao X, Wong CK, Lam CW. (2008). Effect of CHO loading patterns on running performance. Int J Sports Med; 29(7):598-606.

Christensen PM, Nyberg M, Bangsbo J. (2013). Influence of nitrate supplementation on VO(2) kinetics and endurance of elite cyclists. Scand J Med Sci Sports; 23(1):e21-31.

Consumer Labs. (2011). Product Review: Coconut Waters Review -- Tests of O.N.E., Vita Coco, and Zico. Retrieved from: https://www.consumerlab.com/reviews/coconut-water-one-vita-coco-zico-review/coconut-water/

Cramer JT, Housh TJ, Johnson GO, Coburn JW, Stout JR. (2012). Effects of a carbohydrate-, protein-, and ribose-containing repletion drink during 8 weeks of endurance training on aerobic capacity, endurance performance, and body composition. J Strength Cond Res; 26(8):2234-42.

Crowe MJ, Weatherson JN, Bowden BF. (2006). Effects of dietary leucine supplementation on exercise performance. Eur J Appl Physiol; 97(6):664-72.

Dolinsky VW, Jones KE, Sidhu RS, Haykowsky M, Czubryt MP, Gordon T, Dyck JR. (2012). Improvements in skeletal muscle strength and cardiac function induced by resveratrol during exercise training contribute to enhanced exercise performance in rats. J Physiol; 590(Pt 11):2783-99.

Donaldson CM, Perry TL, Rose MC (2010). Glycemic index and endurance performance. Int J Sport Nutr Exerc Metab; 20(2):154-65.

Douglas RM, Hemilä H, Chalker E, Treacy B. (2007). Vitamin C for preventing and treating the common cold. Cochrane Database Syst Rev; (3):CD000980.

Environmental Working Group (2012). EWG's 2012 Shopper's Guide to Pesticides in Produce™. Retrieved from: http://www.ewg.org/foodnews/summary/

Fares E & Kayser B. (2011). Carbohydrate Mouth Rinse Effects on Exercise Capacity in Pre- and Postprandial States. Journal of Nutrition and Metabolism. Volume 2011, Article ID 385962, 6 pages

Feranil AB, Duazo PL, Kuzawa CW, Adair LS. (2011). Coconut oil is associated with a beneficial lipid profile in pre-menopausal women in the Philippines. Asia Pac J Clin Nutr.; 20(2):190-5.

Ferguson-Stegall L, McCleave EL, Ding Z, Doerner PG 3rd, Wang B, Liao YH, Kammer L, Liu Y, Hwang J, Dessard BM, Ivy JL. (2011). Postexercise carbohydrate-protein supplementation improves subsequent exercise performance and intracellular signaling for protein synthesis. J Strength Cond Res; 25(5):1210-24.

Finley CE, Barlow CE, Halton TL, Haskell WL. (2010). Glycemic index, glycemic load, and prevalence of the metabolic syndrome in the cooper center longitudinal study. J Am Diet Assoc; 110(12):1820-9.

Goldstein ER, Ziegenfuss T, Kalman D, Kreider R, Campbell B, Wilborn C, Taylor L, Willoughby D, Stout J, Graves BS, Wildman R, Ivy JL, Spano M, Smith AE, Antonio J. (2010). International society of sports nutrition position stand: caffeine and performance. J Int Soc Sports Nutr; 7(1):5.

Gonzalez JT, Stevenson EJ. (2012). New perspectives on nutritional interventions to augment lipid utilisation during exercise. Br J Nutr; 107(3):339-49.

Goulet ED. (2012). Dehydration and endurance performance in competitive athletes. Nutr Rev; 70 Suppl 2:S132-6.

Gunzer W, Konrad M, Pail E. (2012). Exercise-induced immunodepression in endurance athletes and nutritional intervention with carbohydrate, protein and fat-what is possible, what is not? Nutrients. 2012 Sep;4(9):1187-212.

Hale LP, Chichlowski M, Trinh CT, Greer PK. (2010). Dietary supplementation with fresh pineapple juice decreases inflammation and colonic neoplasia in IL-10-deficient mice with colitis. Inflamm Bowel Dis; 16(12):2012-21.

Hamilton B. (2011). Vitamin d and athletic performance: the potential role of muscle. Asian J Sports Med; 2(4):211-9.

Hamzah S, Higgins S, Abraham T, Taylor P, Vizbaraite D, Malkova D. (2009). The effect of glycaemic index of high carbohydrate diets consumed over 5 days on exercise energy metabolism and running capacity in males. J Sports Sci; 27(14):1545-54.

Hannaford. (2013). Hannaford Chocolate Milk: 14 oz. Nutritional Information. Retrieved from: https://www.hannaford.com/product/Hannaford-Chocolate-Milk/727024.uts?refineByCategoryId=46286

Hannaford (2013). Nestle Nesquik Chocolate Milk 16 oz. Nutritional Information. Retrieved from: http://www.hannaford.com/product/Nestle-Nesquik-Chocolate-Milk/709635.uts?hdrKeyword=chocolate%20milk

Harvard Medical School (2012). Fats Resource Center. Retrieved from: http://www.health.harvard.edu/topic/fats

Havemann L, West SJ, Goedecke JH, Macdonald IA, St Clair Gibson A, Noakes TD, Lambert EV. (2006). Fat adaptation followed by carbohydrate loading compromises high-intensity sprint performance. J Appl Physiol; 100(1):194-202.

Hawley JA, Burke LM, Phillips SM, Spriet LL. (2010). Nutritional modulation of training-induced skeletal muscle adaptations. J Appl Physiol. 2011 Mar;110(3):834-45.

Hawley JA, Schabort EJ, Noakes TD, Dennis SC. (1997). Carbohydrate-loading and exercise performance. An update. Sports Med; 24(2):73-81.

Helge JW, Richter EA, Kiens B. (1996). Interaction of training and diet on metabolism and endurance during exercise in man. J Physiol 492: 293–306.

Hottenrott K, Hass E, Kraus M, Neumann G, Steiner M, Knechtle B. (2012). A scientific nutrition strategy improves time trial performance by ≈6% when compared with a self-chosen nutrition strategy in trained cyclists: a randomized cross-over study. Appl Physiol Nutr Metab; 37(4):637-45.

Howatson G, Bell PG, Tallent J, Middleton B, McHugh MP, Ellis J. (2012). Effect of tart cherry juice (Prunus cerasus) on melatonin levels and enhanced sleep quality. Eur J Nutr; 51(8):909-16.

263

Ichinose T, Arai N, Nagasaka T, Asano M, Hashimoto K. (2012). Impact of intensive high-fat ingestion in the early stage of recovery from exercise training on substrate metabolism during exercise in humans. J Nutr Sci Vitaminol (Tokyo); 58(5):354-9.

International Olympic Committee. (2004). Nutrition for Athletes. Retrieved from: http://www.olympic.org/Documents/Reports/EN/en_report_833.pdf

International Olympic Committee (2010). IOC Consensus Statement on Sports Nutrition 2010. Retrieved from: http://www.olympic.org/Documents/Reports/EN/CONSENSUS-FINAL-v8-en.pdf

Institute of Medicine. Dietary Reference Intakes for Energy, Carbohydrate, Fiber, Fat, Fatty Acids, Cholesterol, Protein and Amino Acids. Washington, D.C.: National Academies Press; 2005. Retrieved from: http://www.nal.usda.gov/fnic/DRI/DRI_Energy/energy_full_report.pdf

Institute of Medicine. (2010). DRI Summary Tables. Retrieved from: http://www.iom.edu/Activities/Nutrition/SummaryDRIs/~/media/Files/Activity%20Files/Nutrition/DRIs/5_Summary%20Table%20Tables%201-4.pdf

International Marathon Medical Director's Association. (2006). IMMDA's Revised Fluid Recommendations for Runners & Walkers. Retrieved from: http://aimsworldrunning.org/guidelines_fluid_replacement.htm

Ivy JL, Goforth HW Jr, Damon BM, McCauley TR, Parsons EC, Price TB. Early postexercise muscle glycogen recovery is enhanced with a carbohydrate-protein supplement. J Appl Physiol. 2002 Oct;93(4):1337-44.

Jeukendrup AE. (2010). Carbohydrate and exercise performance: the role of multiple transportable carbohydrates. Curr Opin Clin Nutr Metab Care; 13(4):452-7.

Jeukendrup AE. (2004). Carbohydrate intake during exercise and performance. Nutrition; 20(7-8):669-77.

Jeukendrup AE, Burke LM, Hawley JA, Wong SH,. (2011). Carbohydrates for training and competition. J Sports Sci; 29 Suppl 1:S17-27. Retrieved from: http://www.ncbi.nlm.nih.gov/pubmed/21660838

Jones AM, Bailey SJ, Vanhatalo A. (2012). Dietary nitrate and O_2 consumption during exercise. Med Sport Sci. 2012;59:29-35.

Jönsson T, Granfeldt Y, Ahrén B, Branell UC, Pålsson G, Hansson A, Söderström M, Lindeberg S. (2009). Beneficial effects of a Paleolithic diet on cardiovascular risk factors in type 2 diabetes: a randomized cross-over pilot study. Cardiovasc Diabetol; 8:35.

Kammer L, Ding Z, Wang B, Hara D, Liao YH, Ivy JL. (2009). Cereal and nonfat milk support muscle recovery following exercise. J Int Soc Sports Nutr; 6:11.

Karamanolis IA, Laparidis KS, Volaklis KA, Douda HT, Tokmakidis SP. (2011). The effects of pre-exercise glycemic index food on running capacity. Int J Sports Med; 32(9):666-71.

Kern M, Heslin CJ, Rezende RS. Metabolic and performance effects of raisins versus sports gel as pre-exercise feedings in cyclists. J Strength Cond Res. 2007;21(4):1204–1207.

Kiens B. (2001). Diet and training in the week before competition. Can J Appl Physiol; 26 Suppl:S56-63.

Kong A, Beresford SA, Alfano CM, Foster-Schubert KE, Neuhouser ML, Johnson DB, Duggan C, Wang CY, Xiao L, Jeffery RW, Bain CE, McTiernan A. (2012). Self-monitoring and eating-related behaviors are associated with 12-month weight loss in postmenopausal overweight-to-obese women. J Acad Nutr Diet; 112(9):1428-35.

Koopman R, Pannemans DL, Jeukendrup AE, Gijsen AP, Senden JM, Halliday D, Saris WH, van Loon LJ, Wagenmakers AJ. (2004). Combined ingestion of protein and carbohydrate improves protein balance during ultra-endurance exercise. Am J Physiol Endocrinol Metab; 287(4):E712-20.

Kressler J, Millard-Stafford M, Warren GL. (2011). Quercetin and endurance exercise capacity: a systematic review and meta-analysis. Med Sci Sports Exerc; 43(12):2396-404.

Lane SC, Bird SR, Burke LM, Hawley JA. (2013). Effect of a carbohydrate mouth rinse on simulated cycling time-trial performance commenced in a fed or fasted state. Appl Physiol Nutr Metab; 38(2):134-9.

Lansley KE, Winyard PG, Bailey SJ, Vanhatalo A, Wilkerson DP, Blackwell JR, Gilchrist M, Benjamin N, Jones AM. (2011). Acute dietary nitrate supplementation improves cycling time trial performance. Med Sci Sports Exerc; 43(6):1125-31.

Lansley KE, Winyard PG, Fulford J, Vanhatalo A, Bailey SJ, Blackwell JR, DiMenna FJ, Gilchrist M, Benjamin N, Jones AM. (2011). Dietary nitrate supplementation reduces the O2 cost of walking and running: a placebo-controlled study. J Appl Physiol.;110(3):591-600.

Little JP, Chilibeck PD, Ciona D, Forbes S, Rees H, Vandenberg A, Zello GA. (2010). Effect of low- and high-glycemic-index meals on metabolism and performance during high-intensity, intermittent exercise. Int J Sport Nutr Exerc Metab; 20(6):447-56.

Love Beetroot. (2012). Healthy Facts. Retrieved from http://www.lovebeetroot.co.uk/healthy_info/#.UTk2lhzkvQs

Lundberg JO, Larsen FJ, Weitzberg E. (2011). Supplementation with nitrate and nitrite salts in exercise: a word of caution. J Appl Physiol; 111(2):616-7.

Lunn WR, Pasiakos SM, Colletto MR, Karfonta KE, Carbone JW, Anderson JM, Rodriguez NR. (2012). Chocolate milk and endurance exercise recovery: protein balance, glycogen, and performance. Med Sci Sports Exerc; 44(4):682-91.

Mahan, L; Escott-Stump, S; Raymond, L. (2012). Krause's Food and the Nutrition Care Process. Elseveir Saunders.

Matias CN, Santos DA, Monteiro CP, Vasco AM, Baptista F, Sardinha LB, Laires MJ, Silva AM. (2012). Magnesium intake mediates the association between bone mineral density and lean soft tissue in elite swimmers. Magnes Res; 25(3):120-5.

Mayo Clinic. (2012). Glucosamine: Evidence. Retrieved from http://www.mayoclinic.com/health/glucosamine/NS_patient-glucosamine/DSECTION=evidence

Mayo Clinic (2012). Organic foods: Are they safer? More nutritious? Retrieved from: http://www.mayoclinic.com/health/organic-food/NU00255

Mettler S, Lamprecht-Rusca F, Stoffel-Kurt N, Wenk C, Colombani PC. (2007). The influence of the subjects' training state on the glycemic index. Eur J Clin Nutr; 61(1):19-24.

McCleave EL, Ferguson-Stegall L, Ding Z, Doerner PG 3rd, Wang B, Kammer LM, Ivy JL. (2011). A low carbohydrate-protein supplement improves endurance performance in female athletes. J Strength Cond Res; 25(4):879-88.

McGinley C, Shafat A, Donnelly AE. (2009). Does antioxidant vitamin supplementation protect against muscle damage? Sports Med; 39(12):1011-32.

Mondazzi L, Arcelli E. (2009). Glycemic index in sport nutrition. J Am Coll Nutr; 28 Suppl:455S-463S.

Montain SJ, Cheuvront S, Sawka1 M. (2006). Exercise associated hyponatraemia: quantitative analysis to understand the aetiology. Br J Sports Med; 40:98-105.

Moore LJ, Midgley AW, Thomas G, Thurlow S, McNaughton LR. (2009). The effects of low- and high-glycemic index meals on time trial performance. Int J Sports Physiol Perform; 4(3):331-44.

Moore LJ, Midgley AW, Thurlow S, Thomas G, Mc Naughton LR. (2010). Effect of the glycaemic index of a pre-exercise meal on metabolism and cycling time trial performance. J Sci Med Sport; 13(1):182-8.

Moore LJ, Midgley A, Vince R, McNaughton LR. (2011). The effects of low and high glycemic index 24-h recovery diets on cycling time trial performance. J Sports Med Phys Fitness; 51(2):233-40.

Moore L, Szpalek HM, McNaughton LR. (2013). Preexercise high and low glycemic index meals and cycling performance in untrained females: randomized, cross-over trial of efficacy. Res Sports Med; 21(1):24-36.

Murdoch SD, Bazzarre TL, Snider IA, Goldfarb AH. Differences in the effects of carbohydrate food form on endurance performance to exhaustion. Int J Sport Nut. 1993;3(1):41–54.

Murphy M, Eliot K, Heuertz RM, Weiss E. (2012). Whole beetroot consumption acutely improves running performance. J Acad Nutr Diet. 112(4):548-52.

Mustafa, K. Y., and N. E. Mahmoud. Evaporative water loss in African soccer players. J. Sports Med. Phys. Fitness 19:181-183, 1979.

Nelson AR, Phillips SM, Stellingwerff T, Rezzi S, Bruce SJ, Breton I, Thorimbert A, Guy PA, Clarke J, Broadbent S, Rowlands DS. (2012). A protein-leucine supplement increases branched-chain amino acid and nitrogen turnover but not performance. Med Sci Sports Exerc; 44(1):57-68.

Nieman DC, Gillitt ND, Henson DA, Sha W, Shanely RA, Knab AM, Cialdella-Kam L, Jin F. (2012). Bananas as an energy source during exercise: a metabolomics approach. PLoS One. 2012;7(5):e37479.

Noakes TD. (2010). Is drinking to thirst optimum? Ann Nutr Metab; 57 Suppl 2:9-17. doi: 10.1159/000322697. Epub 2011 Feb 22.

Noakes, TD. (2003). Fluid replacement during marathon running. Clin. J. Sport Med. 13:309-318.

Noakes TD, Beltrami FG, Hew-Butler T. (2008). Drinking policies and exercise-associated hyponatraemia: is anyone still promoting overdrinking? Br J Sports Med; 42(10):796-501

Osterberg KL, Zachwieja JJ, Smith JW. (2008). Carbohydrate and carbohydrate + protein for cycling time-trial performance. J Sports Sci; 26(3):227-33.

Painelli V, Nicastro H, Lancha H. (2010). Carbohydrate mouth rinse: does it improve endurance exercise performance? *Nutrition Journal*, 9:33

Pasiakos SM, McClung HL, McClung JP, Margolis LM, Andersen NE, Cloutier GJ, Pikosky MA, Rood JC, Fielding RA, Young AJ. (2011). Leucine-enriched essential amino acid supplementation during moderate steady state exercise enhances postexercise muscle protein synthesis. Am J Clin Nutr; 94(3):809-18.

Peacock O, Tjønna AE, James P, Wisløff U, Welde B, Böhlke N, Smith A, Stokes K, Cook C, Sandbakk O. (2012). Dietary nitrate does not enhance running performance in elite cross-country skiers. Med Sci Sports Exerc. 2012 Nov;44(11):2213-9.

Pritchett K, Bishop P, Pritchett R, Green M, Katica C (2009). Acute effects of chocolate milk and a commercial recovery beverage on postexercise recovery indices and endurance cycling performance. Appl Physiol Nutr Metab; 34(6):1017-22.

Pritchett K, Pritchett R. (2012). Chocolate milk: a post-exercise recovery beverage for endurance sports. Med Sport Sci; 59:127-34.

Rauch LH, Rodger I, Wilson GR, Belonje JD, Dennis SC, Noakes TD, Hawley JA. (1995). The effects of carbohydrate loading on muscle glycogen content and cycling performance. Int J Sport Nutr; 5(1):25-36.

267

Reinhart KM, Coleman CI, Teevan C, Vachhani P, White CM. (2008). Effects of garlic on blood pressure in patients with and without systolic hypertension: a meta-analysis. Ann Pharmacother; 42(12):1766-71.

Rietschier HL, Henagan TM, Earnest CP, Baker BL, Cortez CC, Stewart LK. (2011). Sun-dried raisins are a cost-effective alternative to Sports Jelly Beans in prolonged cycling. J Strength Cond Res. 2011 Nov;25(11):3150-6.

Richardson KL, Coburn JW, Beam WC, Brown LE. (2012). Effects of isocaloric carbohydrate vs. carbohydrate-protein supplements on cycling time to exhaustion. J Strength Cond Res; 26(5):1361-5.

Rodriguez NR, Di Marco NM, Langley S. American Dietetic Association; Dietitians of Canada; American College of Sports Medicine, (2009). Nutrition and athletic performance. Med Sci Sports Exerc; 41(3):709-31.

Rossi R, Porta S, Canovi B. (2010). Overview on cranberry and urinary tract infections in females. J Clin Gastroenterol; 44 Suppl 1:S61-2.

Sharoni Y, Linnewiel-Hermoni K, Zango G, Khanin M, Salman H, Veprik A, Danilenko M, Levy J. (2012). The role of lycopene and its derivatives in the regulation of transcription systems: implications for cancer prevention. Am J Clin Nutr. 2012 Nov;96(5):1173S-8S.

Shukitt-Hale B. (2012). Blueberries and neuronal aging. Gerontology; 58(6):518-23.

Siegel AJ, d'Hemecourt P, Adner MM, Shirey T, Brown JL, Lewandrowski KB. (2009). Exertional dysnatremia in collapsed marathon runners: a critical role for point-of-care testing to guide appropriate therapy. Am J Clin Pathol; 132(3):336-40.

Singh M, Das RR. (2011). Zinc for the common cold. Cochrane Database Syst Rev. 16;(2):CD001364. Retrieved from:

Siri-Tarino PW, Sun Q, Hu FB, Krauss RM. (2010). Saturated fat, carbohydrate, and cardiovascular disease. Am J Clin Nutr; 91(3):502-9.

Smith-Spangler C, Brandeau ML, Hunter GE, Bavinger JC, Pearson M, Eschbach PJ, Sundaram V, Liu H, Schirmer P, Stave C, Olkin I, Bravata DM. (2012). Are organic foods safer or healthier than conventional alternatives?: a systematic review. Ann Intern Med; 157(5):348-66.

Spaccarotella KJ, Andzel WD. (2011). Building a beverage for recovery from endurance activity: a review. J Strength Cond Res; 25(11):3198-204.

Spriet, L & Graham, T. (n.d.) Caffeine and Exercise Performance. ACSM. Retrieved from: http://www.acsm.org/docs/current-comments/caffeineandexercise.pdf

Stearns RL, Emmanuel H, Volek JS, Casa DJ. (2010). Effects of ingesting protein in combination with carbohydrate during exercise on endurance performance: a systematic review with meta-analysis. J Strength Cond Res; 24(8):2192-202.

Stevenson E, Williams C, McComb G, Oram C. (2005). Improved recovery from prolonged exercise following the consumption of low glycemic index carbohydrate meals. Int J Sport Nutr Exerc Metab; 15(4):333-49.

Tam N, Nolte HW, Noakes TD. (2011). Changes in total body water content during running races of 21.1 km and 56 km in athletes drinking ad libitum. Clin J Sport Med; 21(3):218-25.

Tarighat Esfanjani A, Mahdavi R, Ebrahimi Mameghani M, Talebi M, Nikniaz Z, Safaiyan A. (2012). The effects of magnesium, L-carnitine, and concurrent magnesium-L-carnitine supplementation in migraine prophylaxis. Biol Trace Elem Res; 150(1-3):42-8.

Tarnopolsky MA, Atkinson SA, Phillips SM, MacDougall JD. (1995). Carbohydrate loading and metabolism during exercise in men and women. J Appl Physiol; 78(4):1360-8.

Thomas K, Morris P, Stevenson E. (2009). Improved endurance capacity following chocolate milk consumption compared with 2 commercially available sport drinks. Appl Physiol Nutr Metab; 34(1):78-82.

Thomson JS, Ali A, Rowlands DS. (2011). Leucine-protein supplemented recovery feeding enhances subsequent cycling performance in well-trained men. Appl Physiol Nutr Metab; 36(2):242-53.

Tipton, KD. (2010). Nutrition for Acute Exercise-Induced Injuries. Annals of Nutrition & Metabolism; 57(2): 43-53.

Too BW, Cicai S, Hockett KR, Applegate E, Davis BA, Casazza GA. (2012). Natural versus commercial carbohydrate supplementation and endurance running performance. J Int Soc Sports Nutr; 9(1):27.

University of Arizona Cooperative Extension. (2006). Calorie Needs Estimates. http://cals.arizona.edu/pubs/health/az1390.pdf

Vanhatalo A, Bailey SJ, Blackwell JR, DiMenna FJ, Pavey TG, Wilkerson DP, Benjamin N, Winyard PG, Jones AM. (2010). Acute and chronic effects of dietary nitrate supplementation on blood pressure and the physiological responses to moderate-intensity and incremental exercise. Am J Physiol Regul Integr Comp Physiol;299(4):R1121-31.

Vega-López S, Ausman LM, Griffith JL, Lichtenstein AH. (2007). Interindividual variability and intra-individual reproducibility of glycemic index values for commercial white bread. Diabetes Care; 30(6):1412-7.

Wilkerson DP, Hayward GM, Bailey SJ, Vanhatalo A, Blackwell JR, Jones AM. (2012). Influence of acute dietary nitrate supplementation on 50 mile time trial performance in well-trained cyclists. Eur J Appl Physiol; 112(12):4127-34.

Williams M, Raven PB, Fogt DL, Ivy JL. (2003). Effects of recovery beverages on glycogen restoration and endurance exercise performance. J Strength Cond Res; 17(1):12-9.

Wilson PB, Ingraham SJ, Lundstrom C, Rhodes G. (2012). Dietary Tendencies as Predictors of Marathon Time in Novice Marathoners. Int J Sport Nutr Exerc Metab. [Epub ahead of print].

Wong SH, Chan OW, Chen YJ, Hu HL, Lam CW, Chung PK. (2009). Effect of preexercise glycemic-index meal on running when CHO-electrolyte solution is consumed during exercise. Int J Sport Nutr Exerc Metab; 19(3):222-42.

Wong SH, Chen YJ, Fung WM, Morris JG. (2009). Effect of glycemic index meals on recovery and subsequent endurance capacity. Int J Sports Med; 30(12):898-905.

World Anti-Doping Association. (2012). Questions and Answers on 2012 Prohibited List. Retrieved from: http://www.wada-ama.org/en/Resources/Q-and-A/2012-Prohibited-List/

World Health Organization. Energy and Protein Requirements. Report of a Joint FAO/WHO/UNU Expert Consultation. Technical Report Series 724. Geneva, Switzerland: World Health Organization; 1985:206.

World Health Organization Expert Consultation. (2004). Appropriate body-mass index for Asian populations and its implications for policy and intervention strategies. Lancet; 363(9403):157-63.

Wu CL, Williams C. (2006). A low glycemic index meal before exercise improves endurance running capacity in men. Int J Sport Nutr Exerc Metab; 16(5):510-27.

Wyndham, C. H., and N. B. Strydom. The danger of an inadequate water intake during marathon running. S. Afr. Med. J. 43:893-896, 1969.

Yang T, Yang X, Wang X, Wang Y, Song Z. (2013). The role of tomato products and lycopene in the prevention of gastric cancer: A meta-analysis of epidemiologic studies. Med Hypotheses; 80(4):383-8.

Zawadzki KM, Yaspelkis BB 3rd, Ivy JL. Carbohydrate-protein complex increases the rate of muscle glycogen storage after exercise. J Appl Physiol. 1992 May;72(5):1854-9.

270

About the Author

Chrissy Carroll is a Registered Dietitian and ACSM Certified Personal Trainer. She earned her Masters of Public Health in Nutrition from the University of Massachusetts Amherst and her Bachelors of Nutritional Science from Boston University. Chrissy has worked in various capacities in individual nutrition counseling, community nutrition, and group wellness classes since 2007. She owns Inspired Wellness Solutions, LLC, a nutrition counseling practice specializing in endurance sports nutrition and weight management based out of Mansfield, Massachusetts.

As a runner, cyclist, and triathlete, Chrissy has a passion for fitness and healthy eating that she loves sharing with her clients. She has competed in events of varying distance, including century rides, marathons, and sprint/Olypmic distance triathlons. A true running enthusiast, her favorite road race was the Run in the Name of Love 5K in California – where she ran the race and got married at the finish! Chrissy is skilled at communicating strategies for balancing food and fitness, and loves working with athletes ranging from the competitive racer to the weekend warrior.

Made in the USA
Middletown, DE
17 January 2017